Navigating Change

Navigating Change

Keys to Leading in Turbulent Times

ONAJITE AKEMU

RESOURCE *Publications* · Eugene, Oregon

NAVIGATING CHANGE
Keys to Leading in Turbulent Times

Copyright © 2021 Onajite Akemu. All rights reserved. Except for brief quotations in critical publications or reviews, no part of this book may be reproduced in any manner without prior written permission from the publisher. Write: Permissions, Wipf and Stock Publishers, 199 W. 8th Ave., Suite 3, Eugene, OR 97401.

Resource Publications
An Imprint of Wipf and Stock Publishers
199 W. 8th Ave., Suite 3
Eugene, OR 97401

www.wipfandstock.com

PAPERBACK ISBN: 978-1-6667-1225-4
HARDCOVER ISBN: 978-1-6667-1226-1
EBOOK ISBN: 978-1-6667-1227-8

JULY 7, 2021

Unless otherwise indicated, Scripture quotations are taken from the Holy Bible, New International Version®, niv®, © 1973, 1978, 1984, 2011 by Biblica, Inc.® Used by permission. All rights reserved worldwide. Scripture quotations marked (KJV) are taken from the King James Version of the Holy Bible. Scripture quotations marked (NKJV) are taken from the New King James Version®. Copyright © 1982 by Thomas Nelson. Used by permission. All rights reserved. Scripture quotations marked (NLT) are taken from the Holy Bible, New Living Translation, copyright © 1996, 2004, 2015 by Tyndale House Foundation. Used by permission of Tyndale House Publishers, Inc., Carol Stream, Illinois 60188. All rights reserved. Scripture quotations marked (MSG) are taken from THE MESSAGE, copyright © 1993, 2002, 2018 by Eugene H. Peterson. Used by permission of NavPress. All rights reserved. Represented by Tyndale House Publishers, Inc. Scripture quotations marked (TLB) are from The Living Bible copyright © 1971 by Tyndale House Foundation. Used by permission of Tyndale House Publishers Inc., Carol Stream, Illinois 60188. All rights reserved. Scripture quotations taken from the Amplified® Bible (AMP), Copyright © 2015 by The Lockman Foundation Used by permission.www.Lockman.org"

To Grace—always there for me.

To Eden—my one and only daughter.

To Efe and Mofe—you guys give me a reason to press forward.

Under unsettled conditions, tents may be preferable to palaces.

—W. Richard Scott.

Contents

Preface | viii

Acknowledgments | xiii

PART 1

Preamble: What Change is + Four Types of Change | 1

    1 CHANGE 101:
        Revolution vs Evolution: How Change Happens | 3

    2 Leadership Vs Management:
        What Does It Take to Navigate Novel Change? | 11

PART 2

Principles of Change: The Fundamental Rules Governing Change | 23

    3 The Grandfather Law | 25

    4 The Law of Systems | 36

    5 The Law of Timing | 45

    6 The Law of Anticipation | 55

    7 The Law of Better Things | 63

PART 3

The Practice of Change | 71

    8 Identify and Remove the Obstacles that Hinder Change | 73

    9 Provide Incentives to Help People Change | 84

   10 Generate a Series of Small Wins | 93

Contents

11 Cultivate a Core Team | 106

12 Make Change Stick (Culture Matters) | 118

13 Use Deadlines and Outliers to Raise the Urgency Level | 131

14 Build Credibility and Become a Leader
    Who Can Make Change Happen | 142

Part 4
Pitfalls and Progeny of Change | 149

15 Crisis: the Siamese Twin of Change | 151

16 Disaster vs Crisis: What Disasters Really Are | 163

17 Near Misses, Close Calls, And Accidents Waiting to Happen | 172

18 Managing the Loss of Critical Assets | 184

19 Managing the Uncertainty
    that Always Accompanies Change | 188

20 Last Word | 204

Preface

WHAT DOES IT TAKE to lead in times of turbulence—in unsettled times—in times constantly buffeted by change? What kind of building can offer the best protection in those times? Do you, as it were, construct a palace or a tent? In his book, *Organizations and Organizing*, organization theorist W. Richard Scott said that, "Under unsettled conditions, tents may be preferable to palaces." In my opinion, his words offer probably the most poignant answer to the last two questions. In fact, inhabitants of rapidly changing environments don't just need a tent, they need a tentmaker's mindset. Figuratively speaking, it's "tents"—a willingness to up and move at short notice, to quickly adapt to unpredictable conditions, and not "palaces"—a rigidity and unwillingness that arises out of an overinvestment in today, that provide the best protection in turbulent times. Navigating change requires people who are always open to new ways of thinking; and who are willing to keep learning and unlearning. It requires people who construct tents, not those who build palaces. Therefore we don't have to throw up our hands in despair at all the turbulence we now face because the key to navigating change lies, not in our turbulent circumstances, but in our own hands—or more correctly—in our mindsets. This is why I'm excited that you've decided to pick up this book. To me, it's a sign that you're most likely a tentmaker!

Undoubtedly, this book addresses a 'hot' topic. Just take a look at the popular management bookshelves and you'd immediately notice that they are chock-full with titles on change and change-related topics like innovation, uncertainty, risk etc. It does seem as if we humans have both a fascination for, and a fear of, change. Indeed, as I pen these words, the COVID-19 Pandemic has, among other things, significantly changed the way we live and do business. But the uncomfortable truth is that a world that has lived through the Black Death and the Spanish Flu has been through this kind of thing before; it's only the scale and velocity of today's pandemic that has changed.

This book is an attempt to help you see that although change is always associated with things new and different—with altering, modifying and discarding the old—at its core, change itself can be explained and managed by paying attention to just a few unchanging principles. In this sense, although change changes things, the principles which govern change are, paradoxically, constant and unchanging. But, and this crucial, this book is unique because it's founded on exegesis—the explanation and interpretation of Scripture. Psychologist Sidney Dekker, in his book, *Drift Into Failure*, said that,

> Exegesis makes the assumption that the essence of a story is already in the story. It is there, waiting and ready-formed for us to discover. All we need to do is read the story well, apply the right method, use the correct analytic tools, set things in context, and the essence will be revealed to us. [It] sees the truth as being "behind" or "within" a text.

Therefore, the material in each chapter is founded on the exegeses of one or two anchor passages of scripture. It's these exegeses that provide both the material and the jumping-off point for everything in that same chapter. Although I certainly want to help leaders navigate the turbulence of today, I have an even higher purpose—to help leaders everywhere see that the Bible is relevant—that what we need to know about change, "...is there, waiting and ready-formed for us to discover." Sure, I use my knowledge of management and my experience as a management consultant to tease out principles of change from the Bible, but, and this is crucial, those principles were always there!

More importantly, I do more than just describe the principles of change; I go further and explain the practice of change—helping leaders see what they can actually do to implement change both in their private lives and in the groups they lead. The book closes with a section that I think is novel in concept: a section that links crises and other unexpected events—which I refer to as the pitfalls and progeny of change—to change itself. In fact, change and her numerous progeny are so deeply interconnected that it wouldn't be out of place to regard them as Siamese twins. For example, where there's change, in that same place there's also often a crisis, and vice versa.

Preface

Using the Black Box concept from computer science, I help you see that implementing change is akin to opening a black box—a slew of unexpected events are likely going to pop out. These unexpected events include disasters, crises, near misses, loss of critical assets etc—all those things that are the real (and unstated) reasons we all dread change. I believe that surfacing and attempting to better understand these often ignored progeny of change is like undergoing a course of treatment with an allergist. The latter is the medical professional who can help you overcome your allergies only by carefully challenging your immune system with small but increasing doses of the exact same materials to which you're are allergic!

Acknowledgments

To Wole Joseph, Myles Munroe, John Maxwell, and Olu Adetomiwa. Four great influencers. Wole Joseph—your passion for leaders and leadership kick started my own leadership journey. Myles Munroe's book, *The Principles and Benefits of Change*, set the ball of change rolling for me many years ago. John Maxwell's study habits—filing, and storing quotes and articles—started me on the road to writing. Olu Adetomiwa's conferences and personal friendship helped hone my thoughts on change. This book is largely a product of the influence of these wonderful men.

PART 1

Preamble

What Change is + Four Types of Change

- Change is that which requires you to adapt
- Navigating change is about correctly adapting to the change that's everywhere pressing upon us

A cat is unaware that night has fallen on earth.
Her pupils expand as light recedes.

—W. Edwards Deming.

PROBABLY THE MOST GRAPHIC and, I dare say overlooked, example of "change" we humans ever get to live with is the change from day to night and vice versa. Nightfall forces us to adjust—we feel sleepier, tend to see things less clearly, and need to withdraw from others in order to sleep. Indeed, one can say that, notwithstanding all our technological and scientific advancements, human life is still dominated by the ceaseless and cyclical change from day to night (or vice versa). But, imagine for one moment that you're a cat; then you might not even notice that monumental change because your pupils automatically expand as darkness falls. To a cat, day and night seem the same. Why? Because cats don't have to consciously adjust or adapt to the changeover from day to night. Therefore, we can say that change is that which forces or requires you to adapt. If you have to alter or modify your policies, programs, actions or thought patterns, then it just might be that you are facing or anticipating some kind of change.

Author and Pastor Myles Munroe, in his book, *The Principles and Benefits of Change,* provides probably the most useful classification of change when he identifies four distinct types of change,

> We generally experience four types of change in life:
> (1) change that happens around us, (2) change that happens to us, (3) change that happens within us, and (4) change that we make happen.

He goes on to describe each type of change, saying,

> 1. Change that happens to us—unexpected or anticipated change that affects our personal lives, families, careers, and so forth.
> 2. Change that happens around us—unexpected or anticipated change that affects our society, nation, or world and that also has some impact on us personally or on our ways of life.
> 3. Change that happens within us—unexpected or anticipated change that directly affects who we are—either physically, emotionally, mentally, or spiritually.
> 4. Change that we initiate—something created or altered by plans we have implemented in order to move us from the present to a preferred future.
>
> We can identify each of the above as a distinct type of change, even though, sometimes, there may be overlap between them.

Interestingly, all four types of change have one thing in common—they force, or require, you to adapt. Change is that which requires you to adapt, modify or alter some or all of your behavior or thinking. Change acts upon us. But it can also act within us and, at other times, it can even act against, or for, us. Notwithstanding, change always requires that we adapt. Navigating change is really all about adapting correctly to the change that's everywhere pressing upon us. That's the premise that underlies this book.

1

CHANGE 101

(Revolution vs Evolution: How Change Happens)

- Two kinds of change—revolution and evolution.
- The *Pregnancy Model* is the biblical model for understanding change.
- Leaders are midwives of change.
- Change is a process, not an event—the process of moving from the old to the new.
- Poorly led change often transmogrifies into crises.
- Because change always births something new, it can be the mother of innovation and invention.

Those who make peaceful change impossible, make violent change inevitable.

—John F. Kennedy

The Russian Revolution of 1917 is the epitome of the popular thinking about change—violent, wrenching and almost completely altering everything in its sphere of influence. It's also notorious for the great suffering and bloodshed it caused. Author and diplomat Kim R. Holmes of the Heritage foundation writes that,

Part 1 : Preamble

Richard Pipes says the Russian Revolution killed 9 million people. Robert Conquest believes that at least 20 million and probably as many as 30 million people perished in the Great Terror. If "unnatural deaths" are included, that number could be as high as 50 million.

But that bloody revolution—and its even bloodier aftermath—probably could have been averted if only Russia's then leaders had carefully managed the social pressures prevalent in their country in the period preceding it. By letting those pressures build up to a head before bursting like water from a dam whose wall had been breached, they wittingly or unwittingly made violent change inevitable.

Change will happen whether we like it or not, but *how* exactly change happens is often determined by what leaders do in the period preceding change. *Leaders are the midwives of change. When they don't lead effectively, change happens as a revolution—sudden, wrenching, and painful. And when they do lead effectively, change often happens as an evolution—slowly, gradually and gently. In between these extremes, change happens on a continuum determined by the quality of leadership in the organization or group.* The writer of Micah, in his description of one of the biggest changes ancient Israel had to face—their forced journey into captivity in Babylon—drives home the point, saying,

> But why are you now screaming in terror? Have you no king to lead you? He is dead! Have you no wise people to counsel you? All are gone! Pain has gripped you like it does a woman in labor. Writhe and groan in terrible pain, you people of Jerusalem, for you must leave this city to live in the open fields. You will soon be sent into exile in distant Babylon. . . (Mic 4:9-12, NLT)

These intriguing words are so crucial to gaining a biblical understanding of change that I would like you to also see them in the Message Translation,

> So why the doomsday hysterics? You still have a king, don't you? But *maybe he's not doing his job and you're panicked like a woman in labor.* Well, go ahead—twist and scream, Daughter Jerusalem. *You are like a woman in childbirth. You'll soon be out of the city, on your way and camping in the open country. And then you'll arrive in Babylon. What you lost in Jerusalem will be found in Babylon.* GOD will give you *new* life again. He'll redeem you from your enemies. (Mic 4:9-10, MSG)

CHANGE 101

Much reflection on these amazing words has helped me see that,

The Pregnancy Model is the Biblical Model for Understanding Change

Models are merely simplified descriptions of complex processes that help us better understand and predict how actual systems and processes work. To better understand how airplanes work, an aircraft designer might study birds in flight. Birds become her models for aircraft design. By saying,

> ... *you're panicked like a woman in labor... You are like a woman in childbirth,*

the writer of Micah compares the change that Israel was to undergo—captivity in Babylon—to the process of childbirth. Stripped to its essence, the biblical model for understanding change is what I refer to as the *pregnancy model*—one that uses the process of childbirth to explain how change happens. Seeing the change process as a kind of pregnancy, leads directly to our next point...

Leaders Are Midwives of Change, and Effective Leadership Can Birth Change without Sudden Painful Transitions

> ... You still have a king, don't you? But *maybe he's not doing his job and you're panicked like a woman in labor...*

There it is in black and white: the job of a leader ("king") is to ensure that the pregnant woman safely delivers her child—symbolism for the work of change management that only leaders can do. The import of this passage is clear: *leadership should* take *some of the urgency out of the change process.* This is the reason for my initial assertion that Russia's leaders in the period preceding the Russian Revolution could have better managed the process and nipped the situation in the bud. While leaders may not be able to stop change from taking place, because they can take the urgency out of the process, they certainly can make transitions easier for their people. In the light of the words of the writer of Micah, American president John F. Kennedy's famous words,

> Those who make peaceful change impossible, make violent change inevitable,

can now be better understood. The "*Those*," in that sentence clearly refers to leaders. Why? Because leaders are midwives of change, and violent, sudden, and wrenching change tends to occur wherever leadership is less than effective.

Change is the Process of Moving from the Old to the New, From the Familiar to the Unfamiliar

By saying,

> . . . *You'll soon be out of the city, on your way and camping in open country, And then you'll arrive in Babylon,*

the writer of Micah helps us see that change is a journey. It moves people from the old to the new, and from the familiar to the unfamiliar. Notice carefully that Israel didn't get to reach Babylon in one fell swoop. She first went, "out of the city," then "[camped] in open country," before finally, "[arriving] in Babylon." In essence, the change that Israel underwent—moving from the cozy familiarity of Jerusalem to the hostile terrain of an unfamiliar Babylon—was actually a process. Change moves us from 'here' to 'there', but only through a process. If change is a process and not an event, then it means that change always takes time and requires patience. All this leads to our next point. . .

Change Hardly Ever Happens Suddenly

> . . . . *You are like a woman in childbirth.* . . .

These words can only mean one thing—*change is never sudden*. Just like it would be absurd to hear a woman at the point of delivery say, "I've only just realized that I'm pregnant," so too with change; change hardly ever happens suddenly. Like a pregnancy that always moves through the stages of conception, growth and delivery, change—even the most 'sudden' kind—is always the result of a process. The *pregnancy model* of change helps us see that although the conception stage may be hidden and gentle, the growth and delivery stages are often more visible, pressing and urgent. Indeed, like any normal pregnancy, *the farther along in the process change is, the more painful and pressing your circumstances, and the greater the volume of resources you'll need to influence the process.* Most people only picture change as urgent, pressing and consequential because they are almost wholly fixated with, or focused on, the final 'delivery stage' of the process. That incomplete view of change is responsible for much of the fear and resistance that colors the popular perception of change. I mean, if I see change only as wrenching, painful and sudden, and as something over which I have little or no influence, then it makes sense to either fear it or avoid it. Wharton professor Jonah Berger, in his excellent book, *The Catalyst: How to Change Anyone's Mind,* drives the point home, saying,

> Take a look at big changes, and they're rarely that abrupt. The Grand Canyon is one of the most spectacular gorges in the world. It's as long as the drive from Washington, DC, to Raleigh, North Carolina, and so deep that it takes over four hours to walk from the top to the bottom. It's so large it could swallow the state of Rhode Island, and so massive that it can create its own weather patterns. How was this vast valley formed? One might think it was a massive earthquake or some earth-shattering event. But it was nothing that sudden or momentous. It was water, slowly wearing down rock, over millions of years. A trickle that became a steady flow that eventually became the Colorado River. . . *big changes tend to be more like the Grand Canyon: a slow and steady shift with many stages along the way.* (Emphasis mine)

Because Change Always Births Something New—It Can Be the Mother of Innovation and Invention

> . . . *You are like a woman in childbirth. . .* God will give you *new* life again.

These picturesque words show us that, just like childbirth always produces a newborn, so change always births something "new." When the 'newborn' of change is useful and better than its predecessors, we say that change has birthed an innovation. And when it's both useful and without precedent, we say that change has birthed an invention. In this sense, we can say that change is the mother of innovation and invention. To be clear, not every 'newborn' of change is useful; indeed, most aren't. But, and this is crucial, change always births something new.

Part 1 : Preamble

A Crisis is "Change on Steroids"

> But why are you *now* screaming in terror... *Pain has gripped you like a woman in labor...*

A woman in labor and without qualified medical help faces a grave crisis indeed. In this sense, and drawing from our *pregnancy model*, a crisis is the product of poorly managed change. Change always upends things, but mismanaged or under-led change tends to allow things spiral out of control until they become full blown crises. This is the reason I refer to change and crises as Siamese twins—where you find one, there you'll often find the other (more about this later in the section on managing crises and unexpected events: chapter 15).

The Best Leaders Help People Change *Before* They Have To

> ... You still have a king, don't you? But *maybe he's not doing his job...*

When it comes to midwifing change, a key aspect of the 'job' that leaders do for their groups is to help their people change before they are forced to do so by external circumstances. In this sense, *leaders are specialists at fixing the roof while the sun is shining.* But here's the rub: as long as the sun is shining, most people aren't really keen on fixing the roof (the classic if-it-ain't-broke-don't-fix-it mentality). So the best change agents are those leaders who can create a sense of urgency in an otherwise complacent and indifferent group of persons (I delve deeper into this in the section on implementing change: chapters 8, 9, and 13). If you have to wait for a head of pressure to build before thinking of making the change, your leadership is suspect. This means that...

Anticipation is a Chief Duty of Top Management

C. K. Pralahad and Gary Hamel, in their excellent book, *Competing for the Future,* said that,

> Top management must not seek to escape its culpability for the carnage caused when it fails to anticipate and shape the future of its industry.

CHANGE 101

The key words in that sentence are "anticipate" and "shape." *Evolutionary change can transmogrify into revolutionary change when leaders fail to anticipate upcoming events.* Leaders who keep getting blindsided by upcoming events are shirking in their responsibility to their teams (I say more about this when I talk about the Law of Anticipation in chapter 6). Anticipation is such an integral part of the midwife function of leadership that I would like to drive home the point with the following case study...

The Case of Nokia

The fortunes of Nokia, the cellphone company, best illustrate the midwife function of leaders—their need to navigate change by first anticipating it. The company was originally a paper products firm that diversified into electronics and mobile telephony. In 1992, then CEO Jorma Ollila correctly anticipated the emerging trends in telecommunications and helped the company change from lumber products to mobile telephony. For the next decade or so, Nokia was the leading producer of cellphones worldwide. But by the end of the first decade of this millennium the company had begun to falter. Nokia, for a while, didn't even exist! Stephen Elop, the last CEO of that incarnation, admitted in an interview in *The Economic Times of India* (06/28/12) that the company's inability to foresee rapid changes in the mobile phone industry—the change of mobile phones into so called smartphones—was a major reason for the company's problems. Nokia's troubles show that a key duty of leaders is to midwife change. But, and this is crucial, midwifing change begins with anticipating it. Where this is lacking, change becomes painful, wrenching and revolutionary—just like the kind that happened to Nokia!

Wrap Around

When it comes to navigating change and crises, the best leaders are always guided by the North Star provided by the following truths.

- The *pregnancy model* is the biblical model for helping leaders understand and navigate change.
- Leaders are *midwives of change*. Change will happen whether we like it or not, but *how* exactly change happens is majorly determined by the quality of leadership at work in a group.

Part 1 : Preamble

- When leaders don't lead effectively, change happens as a revolution. And when they do lead effectively, it happens as an evolution. In between these extremes, change happens on a continuum that's determined by the quality of leadership.
- Change is always a process, never simply an event.
- Change always births something new. When the 'new' is useful and without precedent, we say that change has birthed an invention. When the 'new' is useful, we say change has birthed an innovation. Nevertheless, not every 'newborn' of change is useful—indeed, some may even be dangerous.
- A crisis can be regarded as "change on steroids."
- Anticipation is the chief duty of top-leaders, and is one way they can midwife change and shape the future.

2

Leadership Vs Management

What Does It Take to Navigate Novel Change?

- Leadership is needed when people have to deal with novel and unpredictable change.
- Leadership transforms novel (never-before-experienced) problems into routine ones.

> Routines can't handle novel events.
> —Karl Weick and Kathleen Sutcliffe.

> [Leadership] is a contingency activity; [leaders] act when routines break down.
> —Leonard Sayles

Recently a section of the roof in my house was infested with termites. Time and again, as the little creatures attempted to make the connection from the roof to the closets in my bedroom, I would destroy their sandy paths. The termites, their routine broken up and not knowing any other response, vainly kept trying to rebuild those paths until the cumulative losses of workers and materials literally wore them out! The poor termites couldn't cope with the altogether *novel* (nonroutine) and never-before-experienced situation in which they found themselves. Which brings us to the question: what exactly does it take to cope with novel situations, with change that we've never before experienced? Harvard emeritus professor John Kotter, in a landmark Harvard Business Review article, *What Leaders Really Do*, weighs in on the matter, saying,

> Management is about coping with complexity: it brings order and predictability to a situation. . . . Leadership, by contrast, is about learning how to cope with rapid change.

Professor Kotter's words mean that the poor termites that infested my roof would certainly have done better if only they had possessed some leadership! It does seem that leadership is most needed when routine breaks down and things become a tad unpredictable. I mean, a well-run factory—with all machines humming quietly—seems not to need any leadership, at least not until something goes terribly wrong. Interestingly enough, the words of the writers of the Bible books of Hebrews and Proverbs agree with the thinking of Professor Kotter. Listen to the writer of Hebrews. . .

> When [After] everything had been arranged like this, the priests entered regularly into the outer room to carry on their ministry. (Heb 9:6)

To a student of leadership, these words can only mean that. . .

The Chief Duty of Management is to Bring Order and Predictability to a Complex System

> *When* [after] *everything had been arranged*. . . the priests entered *regularly* into the outer room to carry out their ministry.

There it is in black and white: *before* everything was arranged, everything must have been scattered, disorganized and disorderly—making it difficult for the priests to work in the Tabernacle. Regularity—signifying predictability and routine—occurred only after the proper *arrangement* of the Tabernacle. Arrangement talks about the art of putting things in order—the simplification of the complex—which is the principal function of management. In other words, management's main effect is to create a system that severely limits randomness and variation, and allows people to simply get on with their jobs. She does all this by planning, budgeting, programming and controlling.

Leadership Vs Management

Management Transforms Complex Tasks into Routine Ones

> When everything had been arranged like this, *the priests entered regularly into the outer room to carry on their ministry."*

The book of Leviticus deals almost exclusively with the often complex duties of the Levitical priests in ancient Israel. Certainly, no priest could have entered the Tabernacle to do anything until Moses had finished arranging the place. That is, it was only after management had done its work—arranged everything—that the priests could enter *regularly* or *routinely* into the Tabernacle to do ministry. Again, this shows us that regularity—routine—is the product of effective management. Professor Kotter puts it aptly, saying,

> The whole purpose of systems and structures is to help normal people who behave in normal ways to complete routine jobs successfully, day after day. It's not exciting or glamorous. But that's management.

Having seen that management is really all about coping with complexity, we can now turn our attention to leadership. In an intriguing piece describing the life of the ants, the writer of Proverbs helps us see when leadership is *not* needed. By division, his words also show us when leadership *is* needed and what value leaders add to their organizations. . . .

> Go to the ant, you sluggard; consider its ways and be wise! *It has no commander, no overseer or ruler,* yet it stores its provisions in summer and gathers its food at harvest. (Prov 6:6-8)

These words offer definitive proof that,

Leaders Aren't Needed When People Only Have To Deal with the Routine and the Predictable

> . . . [The ant] has *no commander, no overseer or ruler* [no leaders], yet it stores its provisions in summer and gathers its food at harvest.

These words mean that; the reason the ants have no need for leaders is because they only have to deal with *predictable* seasonal change (winter always comes *after* harvest). If things change gradually, regularly and seasonally, then because the change is predictable and routine, people don't

Part 1 : Preamble

need leaders—they, like the ants, can do things for themselves. Therefore we can say that,

Leaders Are Needed When People Have To Deal With Novel (Never-Before-Experienced) and Unpredictable Change

> Go to the ant, you sluggard; consider its ways and be wise! *It has no commander, no overseer or ruler,* yet it stores its provisions in summer and gathers its food at harvest.

It bears repeating: the ants—like the termites who invaded my home—can do without leaders because they never really have to face anything new. *Leadership becomes necessary when we have to deal with unpredictable change—with novel events or with events that don't fit our prior knowledge, skills, and experience.* Although the eminent Harvard professor John Kotter is famous for saying that,

> Leadership is about learning how to cope with *rapid* change,

I think, in the light of the words of the writer of Proverbs, it would be more correct to say that, leadership is about learning how to cope with *novel and unpredictable* change.

Unpredictable change—novel change—is change that isn't gradual, progressive, regular or seasonal. Ants are used to having winter come *after* harvest; novel change—having winter come *before* harvest—will throw them off balance! Why? Because a *winter-comes-before-harvest* scenario is something they've never experienced! All this brings us to the question: how exactly do leaders lead in conditions of novel change? Or, more to the point, what skills help leaders lead in times of unpredictable change? Psychologist James Reason, in his excellent book, *Managing the Risks of Organizational Accidents,* talks about three levels of human performance, saying,

> The three performance levels can be summarized as follows:

- At the skill-based (SB) level, we carry out routine, highly-practiced tasks in a largely automatic fashion with occasional conscious checks on progress. This is what people are very good at most of the time.
- We switch to the rule-based (RB) level when we notice a need to modify our largely preprogrammed behavior because we have to take

account of some change in the situation. *This problem is likely to be one that we have encountered before,* or have been trained to deal with, or which is covered by the procedures. It is called the rule-based level because we apply memorized or written rules of the kind— *if* (this situation) then *do* (these actions). In applying these rules, we operate automatically matching the signs and symptoms of the problem to some stored knowledge structure. We may then use conscious thinking to verify whether or not this solution is appropriate.

- The knowledge-based (KB) level is something we come to very reluctantly. Only when we have repeatedly failed to find some pre-existing solution do we resort to the slow and effortful business of thinking things through on the spot. Given time and a forgiving environment to indulge in *trial-and-error* learning, we often come up with good solutions. (Emphases mine)

Much reflection on these words of Professor Reason has helped me conclude that...

Leadership Transforms Novel (Never-Before-Experienced) Problems Into Routine Problems

By saying that,

> At the skill-based (SB) level, we carry out *routine,* highly-practiced tasks... [And]... Switch to the rule-based (RB) level when we notice... [That]... *This problem is likely to be one that we have encountered before,*

Professor Reason highlights what the writer of Proverbs has been saying using the metaphor of the ants: *leaders aren't much needed when the task is routine and predictable.* But by going on to say that,

> The knowledge-based (KB) level is something we come to very reluctantly. Only when we have to... indulge in trial-and-error learning,

he helps us see that leaders are most needed when novel situations stare organizations in the face. Such situations occur when we face issues for which our prior knowledge and experience offer little help—forcing us to build from the ground up, and learn via trial and error. In essence, the best leaders are those who work at the *knowledge-based* frontier; who use feedback from trial and error to devise solutions to novel problems. Once these solutions are codified, they become standard operating procedures for others to deal with those same problems when they recur. Professor Reason drives this point home saying,

> Although most activities within well-established systems will have been anticipated in one way or another, sometimes totally novel situations arise in which people have to improvise a suitable course of action on the basis of knowledge-based processing. When the individuals concerned are both highly skilled and highly experienced... there seems to be a 50:50 chance of coming up with the right answers.

In effect, *leaders exist to transform novel problems into routine ones! By the time leaders are through with a never-before-experienced problem, the latter becomes something which associates can routinely take on and resolve.*

Although, these two different functions—coping with complexity and coping with change—are at the heart of the differences between management and leadership, the truth is that no organization can long exist without both of them. By bringing order and arrangement to complex situations, management simply complements leadership's ability to cope with unpredictable change.

Management Is Needed Whenever Management Is Needed: and Leadership Is Needed Whenever Leadership Is Needed!

An army at peacetime can survive being over-managed and under-led. Why? Because in peacetime the army faces only routine and predictable conditions. But wartime is a different matter—a time of great unpredictability and rapid change—that requires huge doses of leadership. In effect, periods of rapid change require greater 'amounts' of leadership, while periods of stability demand more managerial acumen. Psychiatrist Ronald Heifetz, in his excellent book, *Leadership Without Easy Answers*, differentiates *technical* problems which don't require leadership from *non-technical* ones which do, saying,

> These problems are *technical in* the sense that we know already how to respond to them. Often, they can only be accomplished with mastery and ingenuity. They are not easy, nor are they unimportant. Their solutions frequently save lives and require great organizational effort. These problems are technical because the necessary

Leadership Vs Management

knowledge about them already has been digested and put in the form of a legitimized set of known organizational procedures guiding what to do and role authorizations guiding who should do it. . . .For many problems, however, no adequate response has yet been developed. . . No clear expertise can be found, no single sage has general credibility, no established procedure will suffice. These are [problems] that call for *leadership*. (Emphasis mine)

Unlike many people who go to the extreme of glorifying leadership and putting down management, these wise words put everything in perspective and help us see that leadership is important when it's most needed—when we face novel and unpredictable change. All of which brings us to the question. . .

WHAT KIND OF LEADERSHIP CAN BEST NAVIGATE NOVEL CHANGE?

- External change always demands internal change.
- External change demands that you change from the leader-as-shepherd to the leader-as-mother-eagle.

If, as we've seen, leadership is the key to successfully coping with change and, if there are many models of leadership, the question becomes: what model of leadership best helps people cope with change? Or, more to the point, what particular qualities distinguish the leader who successfully navigates change? As I read Ronald Heifetz and Donald Laurie's illuminating Harvard Business Review article, *The Work of Leadership*, I stumbled on an answer. . .

> Adaptive change is distressing for people going through it. They need to take on new roles, new relationships, new values, new behaviors and new approaches to work. . . *Rather than protecting people from outside threats, leaders should allow them to feel the pinch of reality in order to stimulate them to react.* (Emphasis mine)

Coping successfully with change demands that you,

> take on new. . . approaches to work. . . Rather than protecting people from outside threats, leaders should make them feel the pinch of reality,

PART 1 : PREAMBLE

This means that leaders who successfully make change happen must move from a leadership model that's essentially protective to one that's more transformational. Interestingly, the words of the writer of Deuteronomy agree with that line of thinking,

> As an eagle stirs up its nest, Hovers over its young, Spreading out its wings, taking them up, Carrying them on its wings, So the Lord alone led him, And there was no foreign god with him. (Deut 32:11-12, NKJV)

Leaders Who Navigate Change must First Change Hats—Go From Leader-As-Shepherd to Leader-As-Mother-Eagle

Like an eagle stirs her nest...

There it is in black and white: when it's time for the eaglets to make the transition to adulthood, momma eagle

...stirs her nest,

turning a cozy, protective and warm place into an uncomfortable one—and providing the eaglets with the incentive to leave. In other words, before the mother eagle can make change happen for her eaglets, she must first change hats. She must change her leadership model from one that's essentially protective to one that's overly transformational. External change always demands internal change. Most of us are conversant with the picture of the leader as a shepherd: indeed, that model of leadership is so conventional and pervasive that it would be surprising to see people who think there are other models. But these words of the writer of Deuteronomy show us another—less well known model of leadership—the leader-as-mother-eagle. While the leader-as-shepherd seeks to protect followers from change, the leader-as-mother-eagle does the opposite and prepares them for it (indeed, some might even go as far as saying that she incites the eaglets to change!). The former is conservative and unwilling to rock the boat, while the latter is transformational—actively rocking the boat. These words of the writer of Deuteronomy are a metaphor for the change that must first occur in the mindset of persons who want to successfully lead change. They also show us that God certainly practices 'adaptive leadership'—although he does it with one caveat: he, like the mother eagle, knows just when the eaglet (associate) is ready to face and make the change. Until then, he keeps the eaglet in the comfort of the nest, away from

> . . . the pinch of reality. . .

Leaders Who Navigate Change Identify And Remove The Obstacles In Their Current Environment That Prevent People From Changing

> *Like an eagle stirs her nest. . .*

When it comes to change, the mother eagle is *environmentally competent*. How so? Because her very first action is to alter the environment in which the eaglets live. By vigorously flapping her wings and hovering over the nest, she dislodges the soft downs feathers that cushion the nest, feathers which make the nest a cozy place from which the eaglets would deign to leave. As long as the nest is cozy and unmodified, the baby eagles are unlikely to want to make the change. In essence, making change happen requires you to always keep in mind the words of Wharton professor Jonah Berger,

> What is it about the current situation that is preventing, or can prevent, people from making this change?

When it comes to change, people instinctively give first place to things in the future, things like vision, strategy etc. But the words of the writer of Deuteronomy help us see that that kind of thinking may just be jumping the gun or putting the cart before the horse. Again, change expert Jonah Berger, in his excellent book, *The Catalyst: How to Change Anyone's Mind*, drives the point home, saying,

> . . . there is a better way to generate change. It's not about pushing harder. And it's not about being more convincing or a better persuader. These tactics might work once in a while, but more often than not they just lead people to up their defenses. Instead, it's about being a catalyst—changing minds by *removing roadblocks* and *lowering the barriers that keep people from taking action*. (Emphases mine)

The whole essence of the leader-as-mother-eagle model is to identify what factors in the current environment are preventing people from making the change they need to make. Tweaking, modifying or altering the environment in some way—what I call *environmental engineering*—is often the first step to helping people change.

Leaders Who Make Change Happen Provide Their People with Incentives

> *. . . Spreading out its wings, taking them up, Carrying them on its wings. . .*

After removing the environmental obstacles (disincentives) that prevent her fledglings from making the transition to adulthood, momma eagle turns on the charm—spreading out her wings to the now more receptive eaglets to hop on. The eaglets who hop aboard can now be taught the adult skills of flying unaided. While leaders begin by removing the obstacles that bar people from making the needed change, the other side of the coin is that they must also provide incentives to help move people in the direction of change.

Wrap Around

Leaders are most needed when people have to deal with novel never-before-experienced change. They exist to transform novel problems into ones that associates can routinely tackle. This means that,

1. When change is imminent and necessary, leaders must change from the *leader-as-shepherd model* (which is essentially protective) to the *leader-as-mother-eagle model* (which prepares followers for change and gently pushes them to face new realities). The former is conservative, while the latter is transformational.

2. The best leaders are "environmentally competent"—they quickly identify and remove the factors in the social and physical environment that can hinder their people from changing.

3. When it comes to change, incentives are everything. Incentives empower people and give them energy to implement change.

4. The reason leaders must provide the right incentives is, you guessed right, people have a natural disincentive—inertia—that holds them back from changing (more on inertia in chapter 8).

5. Leaders who successfully make change happen are those who craft the right incentives for their people.

PART 2

Principles of Change

The Fundamental Rules Governing Change

WITH TERMS LIKE 'UNCHANGEABLE priesthood', 'better promises', 'a more excellent ministry', and 'a better covenant', the book of Hebrews reeks of change, improvement and innovation. In it we see Jehovah, the Leader of leaders, masterfully orchestrate change—the change from the old covenant to the new covenant. Indeed, we also see him innovating—making things better and making better things. Surely, the astute leader can learn a thing or two from this Leader of leaders! Probably the greatest change ever initiated by God is the change from old covenant (with its Levitical priesthood) to new covenant (with Jesus as High Priest). That change is the basis of the Christian faith. The reasons for that change and the methods God used to successfully orchestrate it—what I call "laws"—can be gleaned from an inspired study of the book of Hebrews. This section helps leaders see the "laws" that guided that change; "laws" that can also help them navigate change today. In each chapter, I first introduce a Law of Change, then I go ahead to write a, "Staying on the Right Side of the Law" subhead that helps you better understand how to put the law in question to work in your own life. Each chapter also has a real life case study to help you see the law at work in the lives of real people. Finally, I close each chapter with a "Wrap Around," a summary of the key lessons that you should take away.

3

The Grandfather Law

- Change will always happen on planet Earth.
- The best leaders always expect change.
- The chief effect of change is to replace the 'old' with the 'new'.
- Change is that which requires us to adapt.
- Leaders who commit to learning and unlearning are more likely to stay on the right side of the Grandfather Law.

Change is [the] principle of life.

—MYLES MUNROE

GRANDFATHERS, IN PATRIARCHAL CULTURES, are often regarded as venerable progenitors of a family. To draw from the field of constitutional law, grandfathers are like grundnorms—the ultimate foundational principles on which everything else rests. If so, the following words of the writer of Hebrews, rightly divided, reveal what I choose to call the Grandfather Law of change,

> If the first covenant had been faultless, there would have been no need for a second covenant to replace it. (Heb 8:7, NLT)

This short, but pungent sentence means that,

PART 2 : PRINCIPLES OF CHANGE

Change is the Principle of Life

To help you better understand this passage of Scripture, I have paraphrased it like this,

> If the first covenant had been perfect and without fault, then there would have been no need to changeover to the second covenant.

In simple terms, the reason God changed from old covenant to new covenant was because the old was faulty. Extending that line of thinking leads directly to the Grandfather Law: since there's nothing perfect or faultless on planet Earth, it follows that change will *always* happen in this realm in which we now live! In essence, change is the principle of life. Change will always take place whether we like it or not. Leaders who take the Grandfather Law to heart have taken the very first step on the road to successfully navigating change.

The Major Effect of Change is to Usher in the New and Consign the Old to History, Oblivion, and Disuse

All this brings us to another question; if change is the principle of life; a thing from whose effects we can never hope to escape, then what exactly is the effect of change in our lives? That weighty question is best answered by looking at a much overlooked change happening daily in our lives—day and night. Probably the most taken-for-granted change in the human experience is the cyclical change from day to night. Although, the advent of technology has made that change look mundane to us humans, to animals in the wild, the change from day to night and vice versa is not only the mother of all change, it's also often a matter of life and death. Why? Because that ever present change forces the animals to adapt or die. Quality pioneer W. Edwards Deming, in his book, *The New Economics for Industry, Government and Education*, drives the point home, saying,

> A cat is unaware that night has fallen on the earth. Her pupils expand as light recedes.

His words mean that a cat is unaware of the change from day to night because it doesn't have to consciously exert energy to adapt—its pupils automatically adapt to that landmark change.

Dr. Deming's words help us see that the signal effect of change is that it always "forces" or requires us to adapt or alter our methods, actions or ways of thinking. Therefore, one can say that *the major effect of change is to usher in the new by "forcing" us to alter, modify or even abandon old behaviors, processes or ways of thinking.* This is why the writer of Hebrews went on to say that,

> When God speaks of a new [covenant or agreement], He makes the first one obsolete (out of use). And what is obsolete (out of use and annulled because of age) is ripe for disappearance and to be dispensed with altogether. (Heb 8:13, AMP)
>
> *When God speaks of the new... He makes the first one [the old] obsolete (out of use)..."*

These words offer conclusive proof that the appearance of the 'new' is often the signal or prompt for the disappearance of the 'old'. Therefore, the chief effect of change is to usher in the new and consign the old to history, oblivion and disuse. Change replaces one thing—the 'old'—with another thing, the 'new'. Indeed, it's this very effect that's behind much of the visceral fear of change that we humans have because no one in her right senses looks forward to being passed over, replaced and consigned to history!

Leaders Who Keep Learning Are Less Likely to Run Afoul of the Grandfather Law

Adapting or making the right response to change always requires that we do a difficult thing—display or put on new behavior. MIT professor Edgar Schein, in his book, *The Corporate Culture Survival Guide,* said that,

> It is especially important to understand how learning and change work in human systems... The fundamental reason why people sometimes "resist change" is that *the new behavior to be learned* requires some *unlearning* that they may be unwilling or unable to do. (Emphases mine)

...the new behavior to be learned...unlearning...

There it is in black and white: responding correctly to change (which is what 'adapting' is all about) always requires that we learn new behaviors or ways of thinking and unlearn old ones. Since the Grandfather Law states that change is the principle of life, since change always requires us to adapt, and since adapting requires learning new behaviors and unlearning old ones, it follows that leaders who are committed to learning are less likely to run afoul of the law.

STAYING ON THE RIGHT SIDE OF THE GRANDFATHER LAW (DEVELOPING INSTITUTIONAL MEMORY)

As I read Economics Nobel prizewinner Herbert Simon's classic book, *Administrative Behavior*, I stumbled on the following words...

> When similar problems occur, it is memory that stores up the information gathered, or even the conclusions reached in solving the first problem, and makes this available, without new inquiry, when the next problem of the same kind is encountered.

These words helped call to mind the words of the writer of Proverbs...

> The wise *store up* knowledge, but the mouth of a fool invites ruin. (Prov 10:14)

Notice carefully that it is having a *store* of knowledge, and not just knowledge alone that distinguishes the wise from the foolish. Since memory is simply a store (organized repository) of knowledge gleaned from experience, experimentation and research, these words of the writer of Proverbs can be paraphrased thus...

> Wise people have memory banks, but the mouths of fools [who have no memory banks] invite ruin.

In this light, one can then say that...

A Chief Duty of Memory is to Help Us Navigate Change

People or organizations lacking memory are inviting disaster. Why? Because it's the information stored in memory that can help them deal with the problems and challenges that accompany the changes they face today. This means that *ruin often occurs to people who have to deal with the same problem repeatedly*. The key question then becomes: how does having a store of information—whether stored in human brains, written on paper or etched in digital files—protect from destruction? The answer is that...

Memory Places the Wisdom of Yesterday's Experience at Our Disposal Today

Solving problems requires resources, and resources—people, money, attention, and materiel—are finite in quantity and quality. Therefore, dealing with the same, or similar, problems again and again can be a huge drain on resources. Which is why people or organizations *that lack a store of knowledge are condemned to seeing similar problems as new problems, and are unable to use yesterday's experience to tackle today's challenges—wasting precious time and resources.* That this kind of behavior drains resources is revealed by the words of Herbert Simon;

> When similar problems occur, it is memory that stores up the information gathered. . . and makes this available, without new inquiry, when the next problem of the same kind is encountered.

People who draw from stored banks of experience can,

> *. . . without new inquiry*

—without having to expend new and precious resources, solve the problems that change presents. Not so for "fools!"

Memory Uses Yesterday's Experience to Convert Today's Problems into Routine

It bears repeating: change always comes accompanied with problems and challenges. People who have no store of knowledge to draw from often see the problems that accompany change as novel, even when those problems are similar to yesterday's problems. Memory helps handle this kind of situation, turning the complex into the routine (a reason why people or organizations without memory banks are destroyed: the complexity of the problem swamps them).

THE CASE OF GOLIATH VS THE ARMY OF ISRAEL

Learning builds on past knowledge and experience—that is, on memory. . . Organizational memory must depend on institutional mechanisms, rather than on individuals, or else you risk losing hard-won lessons and experiences as people migrate from one job to another.

—Ray Strata

Long ago, I watched as a fisherman fished in a river and was astonished at the ease with which he caught the fish. I mean, with the same hook or method, he proceeded to catch plenty of fish. It amazed me that not a single fish learned how to avoid the fisherman's hook from simply looking at the experience and predicament of its "fallen" comrades! The writer of Habakkuk, using this same symbolism of fisherman and fish, helps leaders everywhere better understand the exact value that leaders add to organizations and groups, saying,

> Why do you make men like fish of the sea, like creeping things *that have no ruler* [leader] *over them*. They [fishermen] *take up all of them with a hook;* they catch them in the net, And gather them in their dragnet. Therefore they rejoice and are glad. (Hab 1:14-15, NKJV)

These words mean that,

Leaders Help their Organizations Learn and 'Remember'

> ...*like fish of the sea*... *that have no [leader] over them*..."

Where there is no leader or where leadership is deficient, people become,

> ...*like fish of the sea*..."

A signal distinguishing characteristic of "... fish of the sea," is not just that they swim around in large groups called schools, but that you can catch every single member of a school with one hook or one net *one after the other!* In essence, one fish learns nothing from the predicament or experience of its comrades. Crucially, the writer of Habakkuk attributes this inability to learn from the past and present experiences of other members of the same school to a lack of leadership among the fish. He is really saying that organizations and groups without effective leadership are unable to learn from the individual experiences of various team members and so cannot "remember" or develop institutional memory. In effect, a key sign of leadership deficiency is the serial repetition of past mistakes and missteps, and an inability to build upon what worked in the past.

With all this in mind, let's turn our attention to the now-famous contest between David and Goliath in the Valley of Elah...

> As he was talking with them, Goliath, the Philistine champion from Gath, stepped out from his lines and shouted his usual defiance, and David heard it. *Whenever the Israelites saw the man, they all fled from him in great fear.* (1 Sam 17:23-24)

The Army of Israel Faces a Giant Problem!

Here we see the fully equipped soldiers of the army of Israel flee in terror from the imposing presence of the giant Goliath (a son or descendant of Anak; Numbers 13:33). Would these soldiers have fled if someone had told them that many centuries before, whole armies of giants like Goliath had been defeated by an Israelite army? Indeed, some may even ask, has an army of giants ever been defeated by Israelite soldiers? The words of the writer of Joshua proffer an answer,

> *At that time Joshua went and destroyed the Anakites [ancestors of Goliath] from the hill country: from Hebron, Debir and Anab, from all the hill country of Judah, and from all the hill country of Israel. Joshua totally destroyed them and their towns. No Anakites were left in Israelite territory; only in Gaza, Gath and Ashdod did any survive.* (Josh 11:21-22)

These words offer conclusive proof that,

The Army of Israel Had 'Forgotten' That She Had Defeated Plenty of Goliaths in the Past!

> *... Joshua went and destroyed the Anakites [Goliath's ancestors]...*
> *Joshua totally destroyed them and their towns...*

The soldiers of Israel under Saul's leadership were afraid of Goliath because someone somewhere had failed to tell them that, in the past, Israelite armies under the leadership of Joshua had annihilated whole armies of giants like Goliath! Not only was that fact lost to Israel's army, the methods by which Joshua accomplished that military feat were also lost. In effect, Israel's army, because she had no institutional memory, had to meet the challenge of Goliath as if it was totally new! This lack of institutional memory—the ability to learn from the experiences of the individuals that make up the group, and to use that learning to confront and solve today's problems—is often the result of poor leadership. Come to think of it, if King Saul knew Joshua's tactics for defeating whole armies of Anakites, killing a lone Goliath would have been a walk in the park. The development and maintenance of institutional memory is a general management function that seeks to integrate, codify and standardize the experiences of the individuals or units who make up the group before sharing that information with other members of the team. In this way, what one teammate or unit knows diffuses across departmental boundaries—a concept known as "boundarylessness"—a concept first popularized by legendary GE CEO Jack Welch.

What does all this have to do with navigating change? Plenty. As I pen these words, the COVID-19 Pandemic has, among other things, significantly changed the way we live and do business. But the uncomfortable truth is that a world that has lived through the Black Death and the Spanish Flu has been through this kind of change before, it's only the magnitude and speed of today's pandemic that has changed. Institutional memory can help solve the challenges that accompany today's change by drawing from the lessons learned from dealing with yesterday's pandemics. Change is the principle of life but, and this is crucial, much of the change we are going to experience in the future will in many ways be similar to the ones we experienced in the past. Therefore, the maintenance and development of institutional memory is one way to stay on the right side of the Grandfather Law. Someone may now ask, "What if the change we experience is novel change—one radically different from anything we've ever seen, how then do we keep staying on the right side of the Grandfather Law?" It's to that kind of novel, never-before-experienced change, that we now turn our attention...

STAYING ON THE RIGHT SIDE OF THE GRANDFATHER LAW (INTELLIGENT FAILURE)

Dealing with novel, never-before-experienced change is akin to dealing with situations where the risk of failure is extremely high. In simple terms, people who deal with novel change must be prepared to handle failure. How? By utilizing the concept of intelligent failure. I define intelligent failure as,

> Failure that contributes knowledge essential to success. It often arises from risk taking, experimenting, doing new things or doing old things in new ways. Like the little child whose many falls contribute to his future ability to walk, this kind of failure builds capacity.

The key phrase in that definition is, "... Like the *little child*." When it comes to dealing with the entirely novel 'change' of learning to walk, little children tend to make only 'intelligent mistakes'—small falls that not only don't threaten their health, but which also help them learn and get better at walking. "Bad failures"—huge big risky falls that have the potential to kill, maim or incapacitate are not for them. Harvard professor Clayton Christensen, in his bestselling book, *The Innovator's Dilemma*, helps leaders see that there are actually two kinds of failure— 'good' failure and 'bad' failure—saying,

> But they're smart enough to recognize the difference between good and bad failures. Good failures at Google have two defining characteristics: (1) you know why you failed and have gained knowledge relevant to the next project; and (2) good failures happen fast enough and aren't big enough to compromise your brand.

Clearly, what Professor Christensen refers to as "good failure" is what I call "intelligent failure."

The writer of Luke's Gospel, in his account of the Infant Jesus, helps us begin to better understand intelligent failure, saying,

> And Simeon blessed them, and said unto Mary his mother, Behold, *this child is set for the fall and rising again of many in Israel*; and for a sign which shall be spoken against; (Luke 2:34, KJV)

Intelligent Failure is the Way to Navigate Novel Change

> ... *the fall and rising again of many...*

For long, these words had me stumped. Not until I watched my eleven month-old son repeatedly fall and rise again as he attempted to walk, did it hit me: *falling and rising again is symbolic of the learning process—the process by which people, via trial and error, master novel and never-before-experienced change!* The writer of Jeremiah confirms this line of thinking, saying,

> Jeremiah, say to the people, "This is what the LORD says: *When people fall down, don't they get up again? When they start down the wrong road and discover their mistake, don't they turn back?* Then why do these people keep going along their self-destructive path, refusing to turn back, even though I have warned them? (Jer 8:4-5, NLT)

These words mean that,

Intelligent Failure Navigates Novel Change By Means of 'Trial and Error'

> ... *When people fall down, don't they get up again? When they start down the wrong road and discover their mistake, don't they turn back?"*

There it is in black and white: falling and getting up again is symbolic of going down the wrong road and turning off it when you realize your mistake. It's also symbolic of attempting something new or never-before-done—the hallmark of intelligent failure. The latter navigates change by trial and error, by trying untested methods and practices, and then checking to see which one works. It builds capacity from failing at a novel task.

Intelligent Failure Incorporates Reflection

> ... When they start down the wrong road and *discover their mistake,* don't they turn back?

To, "*discover their mistake,*" these persons must first stop and reflect on the results of the actions they are currently undertaking. Therefore, reflection is a key component of the learning that is required to navigate novel change. Intelligent failure is more than just falling and rising again. Between the falling and the rising, there's reflection. It's the latter that transforms the 'trial and error' experience into insight. And it's the insight that's of value in solving the problems that accompany novel change. Therefore we can say that reflection is the engine of intelligent failure.

Intelligent Failure Always Uses Small Steps to Validate a Process

> . . . . When they *start* down the wrong road and discover their mistake, *don't they turn back?* Then why do these people *keep going* along their self-destructive path?

These words help us see that intelligent failure designs 'trial and error' situations that help her learn all she can at the *start* of an operation. *If you have to spend a huge amount of money and go for a long period of time before you get to even know whether the operation is successful or not, you're not involved in intelligent failure.* Again, every time you bet everything on one single big step that can, if it fails, wipe you out, you're also not involved in intelligent failure.

Wrap Around

The Grandfather Law states that change is the principle of life, and that the key effect of change is to usher in the new and consign the old to history, oblivion, and disuse. Staying on the right side of the Grandfather Law requires leaders and organizations who are committed to lifelong learning. The learning that navigates the change that the law describes is one that uses knowledge from past experiences to handle future challenges; one that draws heavily from institutional memory. Because novel, never-before-experienced change is also possible, staying on the right side of the Grandfather Law requires a learning that incorporates intelligent failure. The latter is failure that contributes knowledge essential to future success, and is often the result of trial and error experiments.

4

The Law of Systems

- Successful change is often the result of the interplay of multiple factors.
- Seeing the interrelationships between these factors requires systems thinking.
- Systems thinking is a discipline for seeing wholes, not just parts. You are thinking in systems when you see the whole journey, not just parts or sections of it. You are thinking in systems when you think long-term, when you place dealing with root causes over obtaining symptomatic relief.
- Successful change requires scheduling and sequencing. Some things must be done first, done alongside with, or done after others, before change can succeed. The emphasis is on the word "things"—the plural of "thing."

LIKE I SAID BEFORE, the greatest change ever initiated by God is the change from the Old Covenant (with its Levitical priesthood) to the New Covenant (with Jesus as High Priest)—a change that laid the foundation for the Christian faith. When most people think about change, they tend to concentrate on a single factor, the factor which, in their estimation, is most important. If they know that multiple factors are responsible for the success of their change initiative, they tend to be blind to the interrelationships and interconnections between those different factors. That kind of thinking often dooms change. Why? Listen to the writer of Hebrews,

> For when there is a change of the priesthood, there must also be a change of the law. (Heb 7:12)

Reflection on these intriguing words has helped me see that,

Successful Change is Often the Result of an Interplay of Multiple Factors

> *... there must also be a change of the law.*

The cornerstone of the change from old covenant to new covenant was the change of the priesthood from the Levitical priests (who ministered under the old covenant) to the priesthood of Jesus (the minister of the new covenant). But, and this is crucial, before God could successfully change the priesthood, he had to *also* change the law. Doing one without the other would have been a recipe for failure. Why? Because the priesthood and the law are *interconnected*. In fact, the priesthood was not just connected to the law, it was dependent on it. God saw that there was an interrelationship—if you like, an interdependence or interconnection—between the priesthood and the law. If he had tried to change the former *without*, or *before*, changing the latter, then his attempt to change from Old Covenant to New Covenant would have failed! In effect, God had to think in systems before his proposed change could succeed.

Navigating change requires systems thinking—the ability to see wholes and not just parts—to see the interrelationships between otherwise disparate factors. It was this kind of thinking that allowed God know what needed to be done first or alone, done alongside with others, or done long after other things had been completed. Change expert John Kotter drives the point home, saying,

> Without much experience, we often don't adequately appreciate a crucial fact: that changing highly interdependent settings is extremely difficult because, ultimately, you'll have to change everything. Because of all the interconnections, you can rarely move just one element by itself. You have to move dozens or hundreds or thousands of elements, which is difficult and time consuming and can rarely if ever be accomplished by just a few people.

The more complex the system you're dealing with, then the greater your need to think in systems. Thinking in systems makes change easier because it helps sequencing and preparation.

PART 2 : PRINCIPLES OF CHANGE

Successful Change Requires Preparation

It bears repeating; before God could successfully change the priesthood, he had to first change the law. In effect, the latter was the deciding factor in any attempt to change the former. Effective change requires preparation. It requires that leaders invest time and effort to know the case sensitive factors—key relationships, materiel, money etc.—that need to be in place or on their side before they step out or at key stages of the process. *Change efforts often fail because leaders are blind to the interconnections, interrelationships and interdependencies among the various factors involved in the change process.* Thinking in systems means that you "see" everything as a network of *interdependent* components that work *together* to accomplish a *common purpose*.

The corollary of this law is also true: unplanned and ill-prepared change often fails because leaders are blindsided by the interconnections they didn't foresee. The law of systems requires leaders to do their homework thoroughly before embarking on any change initiative. To do this, they must gauge the pulse of their people by using a mix of methods ranging from, 'flying a kite'—testing their change proposal with key influencers to see their reaction—to outrightly allowing the people most affected by the change to make their input before implementation. The key to putting this law to work is information. You need to gather accurate intelligence on what the key factors are, how those factors are interrelated, who the key influencers are, what they think, and what conditions need to prevail for your change initiative to succeed. Notwithstanding the type of change you want to implement, the law of systems demands that you always keep the following truth before you: successful change is often the result of the interplay of multiple factors. Navigating change always requires systems thinking; certain things must be done first, done alongside with, or done after other things. Since the law of systems depends on leaders having some knowledge of systems thinking, the next part of this chapter introduces the topic of systems thinking.

THINKING IN SYSTEMS

Systems thinking is a discipline for seeing wholes.
It is a framework for seeing interrelationships rather than things,

for seeing patterns of change rather than static snapshots.

—PETER SENGE.

Many years ago in north-central Nigeria, researchers were alarmed when they discovered that the black substance villagers used to "paint" the walls of their homes was actually a cancer inducing radioactive salt of uranium. The researchers hurriedly notified the villagers, and were shocked by the laid back response of the latter. Since the uranium salt only killed or harmed people in the long run, the villagers were nonplussed! This example shows just how humans are hardwired to give undue weight to the short-term and to discount the long away future. The writer of Proverbs warns against that kind of thinking, saying,

> There is a way that seems right, but in the end it leads to death.
> (Prov 14:12)

These words show that. . .

You're Thinking in Systems When You Think Long-term; When You Think in Terms of 'Wholes', And Not Just 'Parts'

> There is a way that seems right [in the short-term], but in the end [the long-term] it leads to death.

The way seemed right in the beginning—in the short-term—but became dangerous and life threatening at the end—in the long-term. This kind of 'way' can deceive the leaders whose perspective is limited to the short-term, and who aren't bothered about the long-term impact of their current actions. Leaders think in systems when they think long-term, when they place the long-run over the short-run, and when they see the whole of the journey rather than just its parts.

It's Possible to Obtain Short-term Benefits And Long-term Harm From the Same Action

> There is a way that seems right [in the short-term], but in the end [the long-term] it leads to death.

This 'way' delivered benefits in the short-term, but pain and losses in the long-term. The question becomes: how can an action produce one kind of result in the short-term and a different—and opposite—result further down the road? Management writer Peter Senge, in his book, *The Fifth Discipline,* proffers an answer, saying,

> Beware the symptomatic solution. Solutions that address only the symptoms of a problem, not fundamental causes, tend to have short-term benefits at best. In the long term, the problem resurfaces and there is increased pressure for symptomatic response. Meanwhile, the capability for fundamental solutions can atrophy.

Treating the symptoms of a problem is one reason leaders can obtain short-term benefits and long-term harm from the exact same action. Every time you place symptomatic relief over and above dealing with root causes, you're engaging in short-term thinking and your change initiative is liable to come to grief in the long-term. The writer of Proverbs drives the point home, saying...

> Let beer be for those who are perishing, wine for those who are in anguish! Let them drink and forget their poverty and remember their misery no more. (Prov 31:6-7)

Much reflection on these amazing words has helped me see the following truths...

Short-term Thinking Always Puts Dealing With Symptoms Ahead of Dealing With Root Causes

> ... Let them drink and *forget* their poverty and *remember their misery no more.*

The *root cause* of the problem was poverty, but the *symptom* of the problem was misery. By choosing to drink beer to forget their misery, these unfortunate persons chose to address the symptom and not the root cause. They placed short-term relief over long-term restructuring. The temporary reliefs offered by alcohol offered an "escape route" and helped them avoid wrestling with the thorny issues of poverty and low productivity. They preferred to hack at the leaves rather than deal with the roots of the tree. Although this kind of short-term thinking provides some temporary relief, it also has a significant drawback because...

The Law of Systems

Short-term Thinking Progressively Degrades an Individual's Long-term Productive Capacity

> ... Let them drink and forget their poverty and remember their misery no more.

Drinking and substance abuse as the means to forget one's poverty certainly feel good in the short-term. But, as any discerning person knows, in the long-term, they destroy a person's productive capacity—his health, his economic productivity, and his relationships. The longer a person drinks, the greater the chances that his health and earning potential will be destroyed. In essence, short-term thinking—the thinking that places treating symptoms over and above dealing with root problems—erodes an individual's (or even an organization's) productive capacity. *In fact, it is this progressive degradation of productive capacity associated with short-term thinking that's majorly responsible for the negative results obtained in the long-term.*

Short-term Thinking Can Produce Addiction and Dependency

> ... Let them drink and forget their poverty and remember their misery no more.

The problem with drinking is that, not only can it degrade a person's productive ability, it can also promote addiction and dependence—the person begins to require ever increasing quantities of alcohol just to get by because his natural capacities have been eroded. Because I am poor, I become miserable and have to drink to forget my misery. But, here's the rub; because my drinking degrades my productive capacity and makes me poorer, I become even more miserable and have to take ever increasing quantities of alcohol to alleviate my misery. I am trapped in a vicious cycle of dependency and addiction. Social scientist Donella Meadows, in her excellent book, *Thinking in Systems*, puts it beautifully, saying,

> If the intervention designed to correct the problem causes the self-maintaining capacity of the original system to atrophy or erode, then a destructive reinforcing feedback loop is set in motion. The system deteriorates; more and more of the solution is then required. The system will become more and more dependent on the intervention and less and less able to maintain its own desired state.

PART 2 : PRINCIPLES OF CHANGE

The Case of Operation Barbarossa (Hitler's Invasion of Russia)

Make it short! Make it quick! Make it snappy! These expressions best illustrate the thinking that drove Adolf Hitler's infamous invasion of Russia (then known as the Soviet Union). On Sunday 22nd June 1941, Hitler ordered three million troops to invade the Soviet Union. He planned a quick six-to-eight week campaign to destroy the Soviet Army and subjugate the Russians. Indeed, in the first few weeks, things seemed to be going according to plan as German troops captured a staggering five million Russian soldiers and overran thousands of square miles of Russian territory. But unexpected fierce resistance from the Red Army combined with other unforeseen events to delay the advance of German troops on Moscow, the seat of the Soviet government. All this meant that Hitler's army was still fighting in Russia deep into the winter of 1941. A German Army ill-prepared for winter warfare duly suffered her first military reverse at the gates of Moscow in December 1941. Operation Barbarossa—Hitler's initiative to bring "changes" to Russia—had failed.

Although there are as many reasons for Germany's defeat in Russia as there are commentators, one thing stands out like a sore thumb—Hitler's short-term thinking. Having never envisaged a long campaign, Hitler was unprepared for, or never even foresaw, all the new factors that came into play as the duration of the campaign lengthened. One factor that came to play a crucial role was the early onset of winter that year. Subzero temperatures (often as low as minus thirty degrees Celsius) jammed guns, immobilized vehicles, tanks and airplanes, and caused poorly clad troops to suffer frostbite and even death. In effect, winter became—in addition to Russia's Red Army—another implacable enemy of German troops. To make matters worse, on 7th December of the same year, the United States entered the war on the side of Russia. Now Germany had to fight not only the Americans, but also a Russia that was supplied with guns, tanks and food by America. These new factors which Hitler never took into account in his original plan, and which only came into play in the long-term, sealed Germany's fate. The law of systems had taken its pound of flesh from Nazi Germany!

STAYING ON THE RIGHT SIDE OF THE LAW OF SYSTEMS

Successful change requires leaders who think in systems. You are thinking in systems whenever,

The Law of Systems

1. You Expand Your Time Frame: a key reason many critical interrelationships aren't noticed is because of the compressed time frames within which people have to operate. If your change must be rushed through today, then you just might miss the long term consequences of today's actions. Psychologist Daniel Goleman, in his book, *Focus: the Hidden Driver for Excellence,* drives the point home, saying,

> Even leaders of great companies can suffer a blind spot for the long-term consequence if their time frame is too small. To be truly great, leaders need to expand their focus to a further horizon line, even beyond decades, while taking their systems understanding to a much finer focus.

Like Adolf Hitler and Operation Barbarossa, an undue fixation with the short-term means that your change initiative might get walloped by some unforeseen events.

2. You Broaden Your Information Base: the more diverse the sources from which you obtain advice and intelligence before you begin implementing change, the greater the likelihood that you'll be able to zoom in on the hard-to-see factors responsible for operational success. While most leaders tend to seek advice majorly from their confederates, the best change agents go one step further: they actively seek counsel from oddballs and people with minority viewpoints. They take to heart the words of researchers David Garvin and Michael Roberto who, in their Harvard Business Review article, *What You Don't Know About Making Decisions,* said that, "Minority views broaden and deepen debate; they stretch a group's thinking, even though they are seldom adopted intact."

3. You Focus on Root Causes: if you are a business manager focused on improving sales by merely dealing with the symptoms of low sales (e.g., employing the otherwise good tool of cost cutting) while sidestepping the root cause (e.g., a bad or outdated product), your change initiative is unlikely to succeed.

Wrap Around

Successful change is often the result of the interplay of multiple factors. And, this is crucial, those factors often don't bother to announce themselves or show up until you are far-gone into the change process. Indeed, the factors that only show up in the long-term are likely to be the ones that you can least control— allowing them have a decisive impact on final outcomes. When leaders concentrate majorly on the short-term, they tend, like Adolf Hitler in Operation Barbarossa, to be blindsided by other factors which only come into play in the long run. Systems thinking, the foundation of the law of systems, means that you force yourself to take a longer term view of the situation so that you are better able to uncover factors that only come into play much later in the game.

5

The Law of Timing

- When you make a change is as important as what change you make.
- People determine the success of any change initiative, but timing determines how people respond to the change initiative.
- To successfully implement change, leaders must take and pass the test of timing.

In leadership, when to move is as important as what you do.

—John Maxwell

Imagine that you are acquainted with two different young women—A and B. A is a beautiful high school sophomore living with her family who becomes pregnant—throwing her close knit family into great sorrow. B is a pretty twenty-something who became pregnant after her marriage two years ago; a thing that's a source of joy to all who know her. A teenage pregnancy isn't exactly a cause for celebration, but a newlywed's is reason for one. Two women with the exact same experience. One brought great joy to her family, while the other was a source of sadness. The difference was in the timing. When it comes to change, *when* you make a change is as important as *what* change you make. The writer of Hebrews, in his account of how God changed from the Old Covenant to the New Covenant, buttresses this line of thinking, saying,

Part 2 : Principles of Change

> But God found fault with the people and said: "*The time is coming*, declares the Lord, *when* I will make a new covenant with the house of Israel and with the house of Judah. (Heb 8:8)

When You Make a Change is As Important as What Change You Make

Implementing change always requires that leaders display a keen sense of timing. By saying,

> . . . .'*The time is coming*, declares the Lord, when I will make a new covenant with the house of Israel,"

the writer of Hebrews helps us see that, although God knew *what* change to make; he knew that it was necessary to discard the old covenant and make a new one, even he couldn't do it immediately. He had to wait for the right time. In essence, when you make or implement a change is as important as what change you want to implement. That the 'when' is as important as the 'what'—is the kernel of the law of timing. If God couldn't break this law, and if even he had to take and pass the test of timing (apologies to John Maxwell), then everyone who wants to implement change must also face and pass that same test. The question becomes: why is the law of timing so crucial to the successful implementation of change? The wise words of the writer of Ecclesiastes lay out the first steps on the journey to finding an answer,

> God has made everything *beautiful* for its own time. He has planted eternity in the human heart, but even so, people cannot see the whole scope of God's work from beginning to end. (Eccl 3:11, NLT)

Timing Makes A Thing 'Beautiful'

> God has made everything *beautiful* for its own time. . .

The key takeaway from this intriguing verse of Scripture is the word, "beautiful." When it's time to do something, or more accurately, when it's God's time to do something—the thing in question becomes "beautiful." That would lead someone to ask, "What does been 'beautiful' mean?" The answer lies in comparing the words of the writer of Ecclesiastes to that of the writer of Isaiah. Listen to the latter, as he speaks prophetically of the coming of the Messiah Jesus,

> Who has believed our message, and to whom has the arm of the Lord been revealed? He grew up before him like a tender shoot, like a root out of dry ground. He had no *beauty* or majesty *to attract us to him*, nothing in his appearance that we should *desire* him. (Isa 53:1-2)

Timing Influences Peoples' Response to You and Your Initiative

> ... He has no *beauty*... to *attract us to him*...

There it is in black and white: beauty makes a thing (project, person or initiative) attractive. It affects peoples' response to you and your initiative. In simple terms, *if something is beautiful, we want to have it, be part of it, and help it along* (a natural reason why men respond positively to beautiful women). In a nutshell, when it's time to do something, that thing becomes 'beautiful' and acceptable to others. This last point is important because people are critical to the successful implementation of change. Come to think of it, no change can long succeed if the right persons are implacably opposed to it. But, and this is crucial, timing determines peoples' response to your initiative. The words of the writer of Proverbs drive this point home,

> If a man loudly blesses his neighbor *early in the morning*, it will be taken as a curse. (Prov 27:14)

Did you notice that the "good" ("blessing") intended by the greeter was interpreted by the one greeted as a wrong ("curse")? Why? Easy. Because the timing was off. The loud greeting came very early in the morning when the person being greeted wanted some privacy! All said and done, if people determine the success of your change initiative (and I believe they do), then timing determines the response of people to your idea, initiative or proposal. You can still fail if you do every other thing right—marshal all the right resources and communicate a compelling vision—because you acted prematurely or out of time. Why? Because the right action at the wrong time meets or even breeds resistance. Truly, when you make a change is as important as what change you make!

Part 2 : Principles of Change

TAKING AND PASSING THE TEST OF TIMING

Leadership is the capacity to translate vision into reality.

—Warren Bennis.

Management teacher Warren Bennis famously said that,

> Leadership is the capacity to translate vision into reality.

Not only do his words mean that visions don't automatically come to pass (just take a look around and you'll see many unfulfilled dreams), they also mean that the best leaders do more than simply envision beautiful pictures of a preferred future; they go one step further—they know what to do and do what they know to turn their intentions into reality. In the light of our knowledge of the law of timing, we come to see that having a vision or plan of action to bring change to your group is not enough; you and your actions must *also* pass the test of timing. Why? Because, while people may determine the success of any change initiative, it is timing that determines their response to that particular initiative. Therefore, we can say that, probably the most important hurdle to turning your vision for change into reality is facing and passing the test of timing—what the writer of Habakkuk refers to as the "appointed time."

> Then the Lord answered me and said: "Write the vision And make it plain on tablets, That he may run who reads it. For the vision is yet for an *appointed time*; But at the end it will speak, and it will not lie. Though it tarries, wait for it; Because it will surely come, It will not tarry. (Hab 2:2-3, NKJV)

These words drive home a much overlooked truth...

The Test of Timing is Often the First Hurdle on the Road to the Successful Implementation of Change

> ... For the vision is *yet for an appointed time*...

There it is in black and white: visions have appointed or set times for takeoff and implementation. In simple terms, *the fact that you've received, birthed or developed a vision doesn't necessarily mean that it's time to begin*

The Law of Timing

implementing the vision! If, as the writer of Habakkuk insists, every vision is for an appointed time, and if vision only begins to "speak" or become reality when implemented at this future "appointed time," then the first hurdle to turning vision into reality is the *test of timing*. If timing is so critical to the successful implementation of change, the question becomes, how can leaders objectively know that the time is right and ripe for them to begin implementing change? Interestingly, the writer of John's Gospel, in his account of the takeoff of Jesus' ministry, answers that weighty question...

> On the third day a wedding took place at Cana in Galilee. Jesus' mother was there, and Jesus and his disciples had also been invited to the wedding. When the wine was gone, Jesus' mother said to him, "They have no more wine." "Dear woman, why do you involve me?" Jesus replied, *"My time has not yet come."* (John 2:1-4)

Jesus Faces the Test of Timing

Jesus always knew the "what"— he always knew that he was called to begin public ministry. Indeed, he had already selected a team of disciples to help him in that regard because his disciples also attended this wedding in Cana. The major question at the back of his mind, as we can see from the account above, was the "when"—discerning the right time for his ministry to take off. Unlike his mother (who was also invited to the wedding at Cana), Jesus didn't think it was the right time to begin:

> ... Jesus replied, *"My time has not yet come"*

These words help us see that the hurdle Jesus faced at this point was the test of timing. At first, he thought that the time was not ripe for him to start, but later he changed his mind after his mother insisted that he do something because the celebrants had run out of wine. But the writer of John's Gospel isn't done yet, he continues his narrative, saying,

> His mother said to the servants, "Do whatever he tells you. Nearby stood six stone water jars, the kind used by the Jews for ceremonial washing, each holding from twenty to thirty gallons. Jesus said to the servants, "Fill the jars with water"; so they filled them to the brim. Then he told them, "Now draw some out and take it to the master of the banquet." They did so, and the master of the banquet tasted the water that had been turned into wine. He did not realize where it had come from, though the servants who had drawn

the water knew. Then he called the bridegroom aside and said, "Everyone brings out the choice wine first and then the cheaper wine after the guests have had too much to drink; but you have saved the best till now." *This, the first of his miraculous signs, Jesus performed in Cana of Galilee.* He thus revealed his glory, and his disciples put their faith in him. (John 2:5-11)

Jesus Passes the Test of Timing!

> *... This, the first of his miraculous signs, Jesus performed in Cana of Galilee...*"

Those words say it all: the miracle of turning water into wine at the wedding in Cana was the beginning of Jesus' miracle ministry—launching him into the public eye and giving him credibility with his disciples. The question becomes: "How did Jesus know that the time had come for him to begin public ministry?" Close inspection of the passage has helped me see four objective factors that can help leaders pass the test of timing...

The Influencers behind You

> *... Jesus' mother said to him,* "They have no more wine.

Jesus knew it was time because his mother Mary informed him. Jesus' mother was his mentor—having insight into God's purpose for his life, spotting opportunities for him to do ministry, and lending him her influence with the servants at the wedding. Indeed, those servants only obeyed his instructions to pour water into the empty pots because they were acquaintances of his mother. What does this mean for leaders? It means that a key way to discern that the time is right for the change they want to implement is to seek advice from, and agreement with, key influencers. While final responsibility for the change belongs to you, facing and passing the test of timing requires that, as much as lies in your power, you strive to be on the same page with your key influencers.

The Needs around You

> *... when the wine was gone,* Jesus' mother said to him, "They have no more wine." . . . *My time has not yet come.* . . .

Did you notice that the time for Jesus to *begin* doing ministry coincided with the development of a pressing need for his services? Passing the test of timing requires that you correctly discern the needs of your target audience. Do the people you want to serve really need the services? Do they need *you* to supply that service? When it's time, your offerings will be in great demand by your target audience.

The Resources Available to You

> *. . . .Nearby stood six stone water jars. . . .*Jesus said to the servants, "Fill the jars with water.

Did you notice that everything Jesus needed to get *started*, to turn water into wine—the empty waterpots, the water, and the servants to fetch water etc.—was immediately within reach? When it's time, all you need to get *started* will, in a measure, be accessible and available. Doing a resource audit and seeing that you have enough to *start* is an objective pointer that you're in time.

The Ability in You

> *. . . Jesus' mother said to him* [Jesus], "They have no more wine.

Jesus and his disciples were at the wedding and yet, when it was time, Jesus' mother didn't turn to any of the disciples; she turned to Jesus. Why? Because he alone had the ability to meet the need of the hour and turn water into wine. Leaders who pass the test of timing constantly ask themselves the question: "Do I or some other member of my team have the ability to do this?" If not, "Do I need to get some training or someone else to help with it?" To pass the test of timing, you must do an audit to determine whether you and/or your organization have the skills, competencies, and ability to pull off the change. For those who lead organizations, we come to what Larry Bosssidy and Ram Charan, in their excellent book, *Execution: The Discipline of Getting Things Done*, refer to as 'organizational capability'—-having

PART 2 : PRINCIPLES OF CHANGE

the right people in the right jobs. In short, does your organization have the human capital to successfully implement the change you want?

Herding Cats: The Case of Winston Churchill and the People of Great Britain

> Here I am, after almost thirty years in the House of Commons, after holding many of the highest offices of state. Here I am, discarded, cast away, marooned, rejected and disliked."— Winston Churchill (speaking to an acquaintance in Parliament in 1932)

As I reviewed, *The Last Lion*, William Manchester's excellent biography of former British Prime Minister Winston Churchill, I was struck by the latter's wilderness years (1932-1940)—the period when he was rejected, out of favor and looked a complete failure. Yet on June 4 1940, Churchill literally came back from the dead; becoming prime minister and eventual hero of World War 2. The question in all this is: why was Churchill rejected by almost all of Britain earlier on? The answer lies majorly in Churchill's prescience concerning Nazi Germany—the rising power of Europe under Adolf Hitler. Churchill, unlike Prime Minister Neville Chamberlain, saw Nazi Germany as a source of pure evil and a military threat to Britain. He felt that war with Germany was inevitable and that Britain had to prepare for it by rapidly building up her military forces. In contrast, Mr. Chamberlain preferred "appeasement"—seeking peace with Germany at all cost. Churchill's shrill warnings that Britain needed to arm itself for a future war against Nazi Germany was not heeded by his countrymen. Indeed, he was seen as an eccentric whose personal hatred for Hitler had made him lose all common sense.

Not until war broke out in 1939 and Britain began to suffer reverses on the battlefield, did the British come to see the wisdom of Churchill's vision. In 1940, Churchill became prime minister. His accession to the post of prime minister is a textbook example of the law of timing. His ideas and person were relegated and rejected because the people weren't ready and the time wasn't right. Only when circumstances forced the British to see that they needed to fight Hitler did they accept Churchill. But the story doesn't end there. After the victory over Nazi Germany in 1945, the British people, feeling they no longer needed a wartime leader, rejected Churchill at the polls. The law of timing can be a double edged sword!

The Law of Timing

Wrap Around

Many leaders are so focused on implementing their visions for change that they forget that change is made for humans and not the other way around. The law of timing puts things in perspective: when you make a change is as important as what change you make. In other words, how people respond can make or break your change initiative. In simple terms, *while people determine the success of your change initiative, timing determines their response to it. Attempting to rally or win over people who aren't ready can be as frustrating as herding cats.* This often ignored truth has helped me coin what I refer to as, the '5Rs' of the law of timing,

- When the time is *Right,*
- Your people are *Ready,*
- Your action/vision is *Relevant,*
- You begin to obtain the *Resources* you require and,
- You begin to see *Results.*

"5R" thinking can provide an objective method for assessing whether your change initiative passes the test of timing. How do I mean? If you (like Jesus at the onset of His ministry) get the timing right, then it means that your action or vision is relevant to the people you lead. A timely and relevant vision tends to attract support and receive a helping hand from others—things which help increase the volume of resources (people, money and materiel) at your disposal, and help you achieve more results and win credibility from fence sitters and naysayers. No matter what change or action you want to undertake, you need to answer the following questions:

1. Who are the key influencers in the project, and what do they think of your project?
2. What needs are you really trying to serve with your initiative, and does the market need you to serve those needs?
3. What resources are currently available to you to execute this project?
4. Do you or members of your team have the requisite skills and abilities to implement this change?

Write down your answers to these questions. If you don't have the requisite skills, you may need to delay your project and build capacity by

Part 2 : Principles of Change

training etc. In all, applying these principles can help you pass the test of timing.

6

The Law of Anticipation

- Emerging, previously hidden or newly detected needs are the drivers of change and innovation. They are like the needle of a compass, pointing out the likely direction of future change.
- As long as there is a need or want in the lives of constituents and customers that's not being fully served by today's operations, there will be pressure for change.
- The Law of Anticipation demands that the smart leader and her team take some time and make some effort to discern what needs remain unmet or under-served in the lives of constituents and customers.

ONE OF THE HOTTEST phrases in the world of business today is, "What's new, what's next and how can I get there first?" That phrase encapsulates our, I daresay, healthy preoccupation with the futures of our respective industries or vocations. That phrase can also be reformulated more plainly as the question, "In which direction will change most likely occur, and how can I know it before it happens?" Management consultant Ram Charan, in his book, *Know How: The 8 Skills that Separate People Who Perform From Those Who Don't*, offers probably the most elegant answer to the last question, saying,

> Only by looking out far over the horizon and taking into account developing trends that may not seem directly relevant now, can you really. . . prepare for rapid change. . .

In effect, anticipation—looking far out into the horizon *and* taking into account developing trends that may seem irrelevant to your circumstances—is Dr. Charan's 'prescription' for the 'affliction' of not knowing in which direction change is going to happen. His words lead us to an even more important question: what particular factors must leaders keep track of as they "[look] out far over the horizon?" I mean, do they track sales, profit, or number of persons fed (if you're in the nonprofit sector)? The wise words of the writer of Hebrews show us exactly what factor leaders should focus on as they seek to anticipate the future direction of change,

> If perfection could have been attained through the Levitical priesthood... *why was there still need for another priest to come*—one in the order of Melchizedek, not in the order of Aaron?" For when there is a *change* of the priesthood... (Heb 7:11-12)

Much reflection on these words has helped me see that,

Emerging, Newly Detected and/or Previously Hidden Needs Are the Drivers of Change

> ....*why was there still need* for another priest to come..?

This intriguing question hints that the reason for a change in the priesthood was because there were still needs in the lives of the people that weren't being met by the Old Testament priests. In other words, a key reason God changed from old covenant to new covenant was because the former didn't address *all* the needs of the people. God saw that man still had unmet needs. Therefore, as long as there are unmet needs, needs not being addressed by today's operations, products or services, there will be change. In effect, unmet needs are the harbingers of what's new and what's next; they are pointers to the direction in which change will most likely occur. Crucially also, since under-served populations are more likely to have unmet needs, leaders do themselves a service when they look at those groups outside their core (persons at the edges; the so called noncustomers). Why? Because what's next is probably likely to be birthed among them! In plain terms, to avoid being blindsided by change, the smart leader and her team must first take some time and exert some degree of effort to find out what needs, wants or desires are likely to drive the audiences she serves in the near future. That the needs which may drive change tomorrow are unknown to, or poorly articulated by, constituents, consumers or customers today doesn't invalidate the Law of Anticipation. Come to think of it, no one knew that there was a need for televisions until the television was invented!

It bears repeating: the writer of Hebrews is really saying that God had to change the Levitical priesthood (the old covenant) because it was not able to meet *all* the needs of his people. This goes to show that people's unmet or under-served needs and wants not only exert pressure for change; they also, like the needle of a compass, point in the direction in which change will most likely happen.

STAYING ON THE RIGHT SIDE OF THE LAW OF ANTICIPATION (THE POWER OF PRUDENCE)

The magic of discovery lies not in seeking new landscapes
but in having new eyes.

—Marcel Proust

To become a leader who works with, and not against, the Law of Anticipation, you need to learn what the writer of Proverbs calls "prudence." Listen to him,

> A prudent person foresees the danger ahead and takes precautions; the simpleton goes blindly on and suffers the consequences.
> (Prov 22:3, NLT)

If this biblical quality called prudence delivers foresight and enables its bearer better anticipate events long before they occur, then it can help leaders put the Law of Anticipation to work. The question becomes, how exactly does a person develop this almost prophetic quality called prudence? Unsurprisingly, the writer of Proverbs shows us how, saying,

> *Every prudent man acts out of knowledge*, but a fool exposes his folly. (Prov 13:16)

Anticipation ('Prudence') is a Fruit of the Acquisition and Analysis of Information

Comparing Proverbs 22:3, "A prudent person foresees the danger ahead," with Proverbs 13:16, "Every prudent [person] acts out of knowledge," helps us see that the prudent person's ability to foresee an upcoming event is rooted in her grasp of the relevant facts and information. So we can say that, it is the acquisition and analysis of relevant information that helps a prudent person spot trends long before they become events. If you don't want to be blindsided by change, then pay attention to the relevant information about your customers or audiences. What needs do they have? Where are they going for their needs? Who do they prefer to see etc.? As you analyze the data, you become like the prudent man who foresees an upcoming event and can then take steps to protect yourself. Remember, change happens, but it doesn't happen in a day; it happens subtly and daily.

STAYING ON THE RIGHT SIDE OF THE LAW OF ANTICIPATION (BE WILLING TO BUCK POPULAR OR CONVENTIONAL THINKING)

Turn ideas on their heads. Reverse the conventional wisdom, no matter how upside-down it sounds:
"What if we made roads out of rubber and tires out of cement?"
(That question actually led to the development of rubberized asphalt. The rubber from old tires is mixed with asphalt to significantly cut road noise on highways

—STEPHEN COVEY

If 'prudence'—the almost prophetic ability to foresee an upcoming event—is critical to putting the law of anticipation to work, then the following words of the writer of Proverbs give new meaning to that character quality,

> The simple believes every word, But the prudent considers well his steps. (Prov 14:15, NKJV)

These words show that,

The Law of Anticipation

CORRECTLY ANTICIPATING THE FUTURE OFTEN REQUIRES THAT LEADERS BE WILLING TO BUCK CONVENTIONAL THINKING.

> A prudent person foresees the danger ahead. (Prov 22:3)
> The simple believes every word, but the *prudent considers well his steps*. (Prov 14:15)

Taken together, both verses show us another quality of a person able to better anticipate the direction of future change—they are willing to buck tradition and conventional thinking. The simpleton "believes every word." He totally aligns with the status quo and is therefore blind to new and emerging realities. In contrast, prudence involves a healthy disbelief of received wisdom that challenges commonly held assumptions and beliefs. *While the future might be related to the past, it will always be different from it—the reason why, when it comes to gauging the future, popular thinking is often way-off the mark.* Therefore, being able to learn from others while still keeping your own counsel means that, not only are you more likely to see what others don't see, you're also more likely to see it before they do.

A Word for Top-Management

In his classic book, *Management: Tasks, Responsibilities, Practices,* management teacher Peter Drucker divides the work that managers do into three broad categories—operating management, innovative management and top management, saying,

> . . . *Operating* management responsible for performing the work of producing results for today's business: *innovative* management responsible for the company's tomorrow; *top management* capable of directing, of giving vision, and of setting the course for the business of today and the business of tomorrow. (Emphases mine)

Notice carefully that a key component of the work of top management is to provide direction, "for the business of tomorrow." Since tomorrow's business is often different from today's business, Professor Drucker's words mean that it's the duty of top management to anticipate the future. But, here's the rub, a top management that's too deeply immersed in operations (today's business) will hardly have the time and energy to do tomorrow's business. In essence, being too deeply enmeshed in the thick of today's thin things (as some senior level managers are) is a reason many top-leaders can't stay on the right side of the law of anticipation. This often overlooked truth, and not the complexity of change itself, is responsible for many a leader's inability to correctly anticipate change as the following case study reveals...

The Case of Winston Churchill's Foresight into Nazi Germany's Intentions

As an avid student of military history, I have often wondered why Winston Churchill was the very first British statesman to see the threat posed to Great Britain by Nazi Germany and Adolf Hitler. I mean, why were many of the smartest men in the then British Empire oblivious to the grave and existential threat posed by the rise of Hitler? Why didn't they see the upcoming World War? It was only as I reviewed historian William Manchester's classic book, *The Last Lion,* that I came to better understand the answers to those questions. Professor Manchester wrote that,

> However, [Winston Churchill] continued to follow developing situations at home and abroad. Each morning, he and Clementine [his wife] carefully read newspapers and sent notes to each other... on significant items. *One consequence of this was that Churchill became the first statesman in England to discover that, for a second time in a generation, a strange light* [Hitler and the Nazi Party] *had appeared and was growing upon the map of Europe.* (Emphases mine)

That Churchill was the first statesman in England to discover, "the strange light [the rise of Hitler and the Nazis]" in Germany isn't in doubt. The question, like I asked before is, "Why was Churchill the first to foresee the threat that Hitler's rise posed?" The answer lies in Professor Manchester's words,

> ... [Churchill] continued to follow developing situations... Each morning, he and Clementine *carefully read newspapers and sent notes to each other...*

Churchill was practicing what the writer of Proverbs refers to as 'prudence'—acquiring and analyzing information—a thing which helped him, not only see, but also see before others, the threat posed by Hitler's rise. It's also important to know that Churchill did all this *while he was in his so*

The Law of Anticipation

called wilderness—a time away from the madding crowd that allowed him reflect and think. Winston Churchill's example drives home the point: the best way to stay on the right side of the law of anticipation is to constantly acquire and analyze relevant information. But acquiring and analyzing information often demands that leaders intermittently step away from the madding crowd—from today's operations—not an easy thing to do.

The law of anticipation states that, emerging, previously hidden and newly detected *needs* are the drivers of change. Therefore, it's leaders who zoom in on the *needs* of constituents and customers that are most likely to stay on the right side of this law—as the following case study reveals...

The Case of the Humble Shopping Cart

Today, the shopping cart is the generic symbol of commerce and sales. Everywhere you go, online shopping sites or brick-and-mortar shops; the sight of that contrivance says only one thing, sales! But, and this is crucial, what seems so prevalent and taken for granted today was once "future change" to someone else many years ago. The question is, how was that 'someone else' able to see the future of shopping? Edward Burger and Michael Starbird, in their book, *The Five Elements of Effective Thinking*, provide the answer, saying,

> In 1937, Sylvan Goldman, a small grocery store owner, wanted to better understand his shoppers. In describing the buying ability of a customer, he may have thought, "A person can buy only what he or she can carry." Armed with this insight and his desire to enable his customers to buy more, Mr. Goldman took some wooden folding chairs, and affixed wheels to their legs and a basket to their seats. Goldman invented the shopping cart. Not only did the cash start rolling in, but this innovation also led the way for department, retail, electronic, and home-improvement stores of the future to move lots and lots of merchandise. By just describing what was there, he was led to see the invisible.
>
> ... By just describing what was there [the shopper's need], he was led to see the invisible [the future direction of change]...

These words prove conclusively that insight into the needs of customers and constituents is a pointer to the direction of future change. They show that emerging, previously hidden or newly detected needs are like the needle of a compass—pointing in the direction of future change.

Wrap Around

The law of anticipation prevents leaders from being blindsided by change because it shows them that hidden or newly emerging needs of constituents and customers are the pointers to the direction of future change. Anticipation is always a fruit that results from the acquisition and analysis of relevant information. Because anticipation is, in most organizations, majorly the preserve of people at the highest echelon, it's work is often neglected—at great cost—in favor of the more pressing task of running today's business or organization. Staying on the right side of this law requires "prudence"—the acquisition and analysis of relevant information, and a willingness to buck traditional thinking.

7

The Law of Better Things

- Change - even major change - is often the result of continuous improvement: the desire to make something better or improve upon existing products, processes or services.
- Big changes can occur when leaders consistently do small things.
- A desire to improve the current offering was a key reason God both began and completed the process of changing over from old covenant to new covenant.

WHY DOES CHANGE HAPPEN? What are the forces that birth change? Are these forces necessarily big or small, and do they act randomly or deliberately? Many thinkers and practitioners have proffered answers to these age-old questions, but as I read management teacher Peter Drucker's excellent book, *Management Challenges for the Twenty-first Century,* I stumbled on these eye-opening words,

> Continuous improvements in any area eventually transform the operation. They lead to product innovation. They lead to service innovation. They lead to new processes. They lead to new businesses. Eventually, continuous improvement leads to fundamental change.

For me, the key phrases in this illuminating paragraph are, "Continuous improvements," and "fundamental change." These phrases helped me see that change—even change of the most fundamental and far reaching kind—is often a result of steady and cumulative improvement. In simple terms, big changes can occur when leaders consistently do small things: when they consistently engage in the mundane and humdrum task of continuous improvement. When most people think of the new covenant, they tend to think it must have been the result of a single major operation (like a big bang), but the words of the writer of Hebrews are at odds with that kind of thinking,

> But now hath he [Jesus] obtained a *more excellent* ministry, by how much also he is a mediator of a *better* covenant, which was established upon *better* promises. (Heb 8:6, KJV)

These words not only help us see that Jesus is the mediator of the new covenant, they also show that,

Change—Even Fundamental Change—is Often the Result of a Commitment to Continuous Improvement

The terms of comparison in this passage of Scripture ("*more excellent*," "*better* covenant," and "*better* promises.") reveal God's overriding concern for continuous improvement, and clearly show that he changed the old covenant and brought in the new simply because he wanted something better! In essence, a desire to improve the current offering was a key reason God both began and completed the process of changing over from old covenant to new covenant. The latter could better serve the needs of the people than the former. *The law of better things states that change is often the result of a desire to make something better; to improve upon an existing product, process or service.*

The Law of Better Things Ensures that a Leader's Change Initiative Always Conforms to the Highest Ethical Standards

> ....a better covenant, which was established upon *better promises.*

Since better promises equal better services for us, the reason God changed to the new covenant was so that we would be better served! Unlike the other 'laws' of change which majorly describe the 'what'—the methods by which God changed from old covenant to new covenant—the law of better things goes one step further and deals with the 'why', the reason for that change (a desire to better serve people). Stripped to its essence, the law of better things helps leaders answer the question, "Why do we need this change, and who will benefit from it?" It brings to the fore the motives that leaders *should* have whenever they want to implement change—to make things better or to make better things for the people they lead. It helps leaders see that, if the change they hope to initiate or lead wouldn't better the lot of all or a majority of their constituents, then that "change" isn't worth the paper it's written on. The law of better things provides the guard rails and a deep set of values that help leaders ensure that their vision for change always conforms to the highest ethical standards.

The Law of Better Things Deals with both 'Methods' and 'Motives'

In a nutshell, the law of better things deals with two factors—'what' and 'why'. The former is all about the *methods* of continuous improvement that drive change, while the latter is about the *motives* for the change that you want to implement. Together, these two factors are like a person's right and left hands.

STAYING ON THE RIGHT SIDE OF THE LAW OF BETTER THINGS (CRITICAL THINKING)

> CRITICAL: "Inclined to find fault"—Random House Dictionary

Critical thinking—the term already hints at its own meaning. *Random House Dictionary* defines the word "critical" as "inclined to find fault." Therefore, we can say that critical thinking is thinking that, in a bid to improve upon present operations, questions and finds fault with current actions, products, processes or services. The words of the writer of Hebrews show us that this kind of thinking was central to making the change from old covenant to new covenant,

> For if that first covenant had been faultless, then no place would have been sought for a second. Because *finding fault* with them He says: "Behold, the days are coming, says the Lord, when I will make a *new* covenant with the house of Israel and with the house of Judah— (Heb 8:7-8, NKJV)

These intriguing words help us see that. . .

PART 2 : PRINCIPLES OF CHANGE

Critical Thinking is 'Fault Finding' that Spurs Improvement

> . . . .Because *finding fault* with them He says: "Behold, the days are coming, says the Lord, when I will make a *new* covenant. . .

To make a new and better covenant, and to improve upon the old, God had to first "[find] fault" with the current. In simple terms, God had to engage in critical thinking before he could make a new and better covenant! But critical thinking isn't rocket science.

Leaders are thinking critically whenever they exhibit. . .

A Healthy Dissatisfaction with the Status Quo (Problem-finding)

> . . . Because *finding fault with them he says:* . . . *I will make a new covenant.* . .

Although God himself instituted the first covenant, that didn't preclude him from probing to see what was wrong, or from finding fault, with it. In essence, God had to exhibit a healthy dissatisfaction with his current product (the old covenant) before he could make a better one (the new covenant). *Because critical thinking always exhibits a healthy dissatisfaction with current processes, it's the ultimate problem-finding behavior.* Most leaders are conversant with problem-solving—front-end actions that seek solutions to problems *after* they occur. In contrast, problem-finding is a back-end action that actively seeks problems or weaknesses in current operations *before* they occur. Critical thinking is heavily weighted towards the latter, and always exhibits an inclination or disposition to find fault with current processes and products. By helping leaders see what's wrong, what can go wrong or what can be made better with current processes and products, critical thinking powers improvement and change.

A Willingness to Abandon or Modify Current Processes or Offerings (Planned Abandonment)

> . . . Finding fault with them he says, "Behold. . . *I will make a new covenant.*"

Notice carefully that God didn't wait for the old covenant to go broke before he fixed it. Instead, he probed to find out what *could* go wrong and, on that basis, crafted a new covenant. An if-it-ain't-broke-don't-fix-it mentality is the enemy of critical thinking because it's unwilling or unable to abandon or modify old processes unless or until they are broken. Critical thinking doesn't wait for things to get broken before it acts. It actively seeks errors, mistakes and defects in the operation of current products and, this is crucial, it uses those errors as launch pads to make things better. Most importantly, critical thinking is willing to modify or even abandon old processes—what management teacher Peter Drucker refers to as "planned abandonment."

The Case of the Japanese *Risorgimento* (The Miraculous Postwar Growth of Japan's Automakers)

Nothing typifies the Japanese *Risorgimento*—Japan's economic rise after suffering almost total destruction during World War 2—like the growth of her automakers. Japanese carmakers are probably the greatest example of marketplace success the world has ever seen. Their dominance in the auto industry is almost taken for granted today, so much that many have forgotten their very humble beginnings and the obstacles they had to surmount. Harvard professor David Landes, in his excellent book, *The Wealth & Poverty of Nations*, has this to say about the phenomenal transformation of the once backward Japanese automakers:

> In 1950, Japan made 32,000 vehicles - about one and a half days of American manufacture... By 1960, car output stood at 482,000 units... A decade later, Japan made an astonishing 5.3 million cars... By 1980, it was shipping 6 million vehicles... and had passed the US as the largest carmaker in the world... These growth rates of 30 and 40 percent a year in the face of immensely rich and firmly entrenched competitors will be studied in the future as a lesson...

Going from an output of 32,000 in 1950 to over 6 million in the eighties is an economic miracle! And all this happened in the face of economically powerful competition. To what then can we attribute these astonishing growth rates? In the same book, Professor Landes helps us with the answer, saying...

> How did the Japanese do it? *First*... *they learned to design and test faster:* 46 months in Japan vs. 60 in the USA... to create a new model... They could change dies in stamping presses in 5

minutes, compared with 8 to 24 hours in an American plant. (Emphasis mine)

There it is in black and white. *A total commitment to learning and improving processes was at the heart of the Japanese Risorgimento.*

Today, most students of economic history are agreed that much of Japan's industrial success post World War 2, was built, in part, on a principle—*kaizen*—which emphasizes a daily and incremental improvement on current processes and products. Japanese automakers simply embraced the law of better things. The good news is that this law, like all the other laws of change, is really no respecter of persons. Anyone who stays on its right side will engage in the continuous improvement that leads to fundamental change. Whatever, effective leaders cultivate a healthy dissatisfaction with today's products and offerings (no matter how successful they currently are in the marketplace) and constantly tinker with their systems in order to improve them. Complacency (I will say more about this in the section on implementing change)—an insidious satisfaction with today's operations—always brings an organization smack dab against the law of Better Things.

But critical thinking is more than just a commitment to continuous improvement, a healthy dissatisfaction with current processes or a willingness to abandon current offerings. At its core, it's an attitude that's ready to question conventional thinking and buck tradition. The following words of the writer of Proverbs help us see this central quality of critical thinking,

> The simple believes every word; but the prudent man looketh well to his going." (Prov 14:15, KJV)

These words mean that,

Critical Thinking Regularly Questions Conventional Thinking

The simpleton

> believes every word.

In other words, she *uncritically* accepts received wisdom and is therefore *unable to see alternatives to current practices*. In contrast, 'prudence' involves a healthy disbelief of received wisdom which respectfully challenges commonly held beliefs, assumptions and practices—

> . . . the prudent man looketh well to his going.

—even when those beliefs are held by so called 'authorities'. In this way, prudence begins to, not only 'see', but to also see beforehand, the things that others are blind to. In doing this, prudence becomes what management scholars call critical thinking—which respectfully questions and challenges commonly held beliefs and traditions. This kind of contrarian thinking is key to seeing what the masses overlook or don't see at all. Adult education expert Stephen Brookfield, said that,

> [Critical thinking is] the ability to imagine alternatives to one's current ways of thinking and living. . . [and] often entails a deliberate break with rational modes of thinking in order to prompt forward leaps in creativity.

Critical thinking gives a huge boost to creativity. I once saw, on a friend's Facebook page, a widely accepted saying, "Blowing out someone else's candle will not make yours shine brighter." Most people uncritically accept this saying, but come to think of it; what if my candle is dim and flickering, will blowing out yours not make mine seem to shine brighter? That's how critical thinking works—it questions popular thinking and received wisdom, and is willing to modify or abandon "settled" ways of thinking and operating. It's these attitudes and actions that are at the heart of the law of better things.

Wrap Around

The law of better things states that fundamental change is often the result of a commitment to the humdrum and everyday process of continuous improvement. But a commitment to continuous improvement itself is founded on the bedrock of critical thinking—a healthy dissatisfaction with the status quo that shows up as a commitment to learning and improving, and a willingness to abandon current offerings. The law of better things works best where leaders jettison the if-it-ain't-broke-don't-fix-it mentality.

PART 3

The Practice of Change

It should be borne in mind that there is nothing more difficult to arrange, more doubtful of success and more dangerous to carry through than initiating changes. The innovator makes enemies of all those who prospered under the old order and only lukewarm support is forthcoming from those who would prosper under the new.

—NICCOLO MACHIAVELLI

VISIONS OF CHANGE ARE free and certainly easy to conjure, but implementing change is where the proverbial rubber meets the road. As the above words of Machiavelli imply, implementing change is tough for a variety of reasons, chief of which is the people factor. For change to be successfully implemented, leaders must carefully address the eight different factors outlined in this section.

8

Identify and Remove the Obstacles that Hinder Change

THE BEST LEADERS KNOW that they must,

- Overcome inertia
- Combat complacency

The implementation of any kind of major change requires action from a large number of people.

—JOHN KOTTER

WHEN IT COMES TO implementing change, most people think that it's "things immaterial" (vision, hope, strategy etc.) and "things material," (money and other material resources) that matter most. They tend to overlook or downplay "things people," or the role of people. Italian philosopher Niccolo Machiavelli, in his book, *The Prince*, takes a hammer to that kind of thinking, saying,

> It should be borne in mind that there is nothing more difficult to arrange, more doubtful of success and more dangerous to carry through than initiating changes. The innovator makes enemies of all those who prospered under the old order and only lukewarm support is forthcoming from those who would prosper under the new.

Part 3 : The Practice of Change

Notice carefully that nowhere in Machiavelli's now-famous statement is mention made of the amount of money and other material resources possessed by the leader ("innovator"), the relevance of her vision or the wisdom of her strategic plans. Machiavelli majorly—and I daresay, rightly— ascribes the difficulties associated with implementing change ("initiating changes") to problems associated with having to work with or through other people. In effect, people problems, not technical or resource problems are the major stumbling blocks on the road to implementing change. Academics Chip and Dan Heath, in their illuminating book, *Switch: How to Change Things When Change is Hard,* underscore the point, saying,

> For anything to change, someone has to start acting differently. . . Ultimately, all change efforts boil down.to the same mission: Can you get people to start behaving in a new way?

Leaders who take an overly technical view of the change process tend to say, "If only I had more money/time/material assets, I would be able to see this change through," while those who take a more balanced view tend to say, "Even with all the money/time/material assets available to me, seeing this change through requires that I lead people more effectively." The technical view causes leaders to concentrate most of their effort on casting vision and developing a winning strategy to make change a reality— things that are necessary, but grossly insufficient to successfully implement change. The words of the writer of Deuteronomy, using the symbolism of a mother eagle helping her eaglets make the transition to adulthood, drive the point home,

> As an eagle stirs up its nest, Hovers over its young, Spreading out its wings, taking them up, Carrying them on its wings, So the Lord alone led him, And there was no foreign god with him. (Deut 32:11-12, NKJV)

These symbolic words mean that,

People Are Hardwired to Resist Change

As an eagle stirs up its nest. . .

The change was natural (I mean, it's eaglets that become eagles). The change was timely (the time had come for the eaglets to make the transition to adulthood). The change was well resourced (mother eagle had all it took).

Identify and Remove the Obstacles that Hinder Change

The change was relevant and necessary. Yet the eaglets didn't want to make the change; mother eagle needed to coax them into it by stirring the nest. This is symbolic of the tendency of humans to resist change—even when that change is timely, relevant and necessary. Leadership that successfully implements change is one that's both acutely aware of, and very comfortable with, this uncomfortable truth; people don't like change! It's the real reason 'people factors' are the most important variables in the equation for implementing change.

Identifying and Removing the Obstacles that Prevent People From Changing is a Key Step on the Road to Successfully Implementing Change

As an eagle stirs up its nest. . .

Momma eagle, using materials made from twigs and thorns, builds her nest on a crag or high place. She then lines the nest with soft downs feathers taken from her breast—making for a cozy residence. When it's time for the eaglets to make the transition to adulthood, mother eagle ". . . stirs up the nest," by hovering over it and flapping her wings—causing the soft downs feathers which overlie the nest to be shaken and removed, and revealing the underlying thorns and twigs. In effect, "stirring up the nest," turns a once cozy and protective place into an uncomfortable one, and provides the eaglets with an incentive to make the change and leave the nest. The moral of this passage is that the best leaders *begin* implementing change—even change that's timely, necessary and relevant—by *first* identifying and removing the things which can prevent their people from changing. Wharton professor Jonah Berger, in his book, *Catalyst: How to Change Anyone's Mind*, said that,

> . . . there is a better way to generate change. It's not about pushing harder. And it's not about being more convincing or a better persuader. These tactics might work once in a while, but more often than not they just lead people to up their defenses. Instead, it's about being a catalyst—changing minds by *removing roadblocks and lowering the barriers that keep people from taking action*. That's exactly what hostage negotiators do. . . Great hostage negotiators don't push harder. Or up the heat in an already tense situation. Instead, *they identify what's preventing change from happening and*

remove that barrier. Allowing change to happen with less energy, not more. Just like a catalyst. (Emphases mine)

Professor Berger could just as well have taken his bearings from the words of the writer of Deuteronomy! Whatever, the key takeaway in all this is that implementing change always requires that you look carefully at the environment—physical and social—within which people operate and identify the factors (physical, sociocultural, and economic) that will likely prevent people from changing their behaviors. Once identified, those factors, like the soft downs feathers which overlie the eagle's nest, must be addressed, removed or mitigated. Failure to address them not only means that they will be a constant drag on the implementation process, it also means that more energy, effort and resources will be spent on pushing change through.

INERTIA

If leaders must first remove the disincentives that prevent people from changing before change can be successfully implemented and, if people have a natural disincentive to change of most kinds, then it makes sense to take a closer look at the nature of that disincentive. In a parable that uses wine and the winemaking process to explain peoples' resistance to change, Jesus puts a finger on the real nature of that disincentive, saying,

> And no one pours new wine into old wineskins. If he does, the new wine will burst the skins, the wine will run out and the wineskins will be ruined. No, new wine must be poured into new wineskins. And no one after drinking old wine wants the new, for he says, 'The old is better.' (Luke 5:37-39)

Jesus' words mean that,

Inertia is a Natural Disincentive on the Road to Implementing Change

> *... And no one after drinking old wine wants the new, for [because] they say, 'The old is better.'*

The people didn't want the new wine simply because they'd drunk the old. They preferred the status quo! And why did they prefer the status quo? Easy.

Identify and Remove the Obstacles that Hinder Change

Because they had tasted of the old wine ("the old is better."). In essence, historical issues—the pull of the past and the tug of the present—served as drags and deadweights on their willingness to change. This pull of the past or tug of the present that produces resistance to change is inertia. As the words of Jesus show, inertia often shows up as complacency, indifference or even hostility to the new. Newton's first law of motion (which describes inertia) states that, "Every object continues in the same state of rest or uniform motion unless some external force is applied." The key words for me in that statement are, "continues," and "external force." The word "continues," paints a picture of timing and duration, and hints that the longer an object stays in a state of rest or uniform motion, the greater its inertia, and the greater the "external force" needed to change its current state. In simple terms, the longer people have remained in a particular situation, the greater the inertia; the greater their resistance to change, and the greater the work leaders must do to successfully implement change. Therefore we can say that, inertia or an unwillingness to change is the first obstacle that leaders who successfully implement change must identify and tackle.

AGAINST THE TIDE: THE STORY OF SAMSON

We see these truths about inertia writ large in the story of Samson—Israel's leader and one-man-army—who could kill 1000 enemy troops while armed with only the jaw bone of a donkey! Samson's leadership has always fascinated me. No matter how many times he singlehandedly defeated the Philistine army, and no matter how many Philistines he singlehandedly killed, not a single person in Israel rallied to his side! Not even his killing of the entire Philistine leadership and 3000 other persons—a thing which also led to his own death in captivity—could convince any Israelite to identify with him! How do I know this? Easy. Because Samson's funeral was attended by only members of his own family (Judges 16:31). The question becomes: why, with all Samson's visible wins, did no one join him in his crusade to end Israel's subjugation at the hands of the Philistines? The answer lies in one word—inertia. Listen to the writer of Judges as he tells the story of Samson,

> And the children of Israel did evil again in the sight of the LORD; and the LORD delivered them into the hand of the Philistines *forty years*. . . . For, lo, thou shalt conceive, and bear a son; and no razor shall come on his head: for the child shall be a Nazarite unto God

> from the womb: and he shall begin to deliver Israel out of the hand of the Philistines. (Judg 13:1-5, KJV)

This passage shows us two reasons why Samson found it so difficult to get any form of buy-in from his people...

Samson Was Up Against Plenty of Inertia

> ....and the Lord delivered them [Israel] into the hand of Philistine forty years...

There it is in black and white: Israel was in slavery and subjection to the Philistines for a whole forty years! Imagine, children were born and raised under the suzerainty of the Philistines. Those same children grew up, got married, gave birth to, and reared their own children under the same Philistine subjugation. The people had continued long under subjection, and had become used to being slaves to the Philistines, and anyone attempting to change their circumstance was going to have to deal with plenty of inertia. Small wonder Samson's miraculous string of victories against the Philistines made hardly a dent on the mindset of the average Israelite. In fact, at one time, a 3000-strong army of Judah even did the unthinkable—restrain Samson with ropes and deliver him to the Philistines (Judges 15:11-15)! The longer people have lived with or accepted the status quo, the greater their aversion to change and the harder the job facing the change agent. Why? Because of inertia. Inertia is proportional to the amount of time people have spent in the status quo.

Samson Was a Pioneer—One Who Begins an Enterprise or Initiative

Imagine you're moving house and need to drag your favorite settee to the moving truck. You and a close friend begin to push and pull the large settee across your living room. In the beginning, it's tough work, but as both of you push it farther along the room, things become a little easier. Welcome to the world of inertia, a world where starting the process is harder than continuing it. By saying,

> ... and he [Samson] shall *begin* to deliver Israel from the hands of the Philistines,

Identify and Remove the Obstacles that Hinder Change

the writer of Judges helps us see that Samson's task would be very difficult. Why? Because Samson was to *begin* the change process—a thing which would see him face greater inertia and resistance than anyone else. Come to think of it, although both Samson and David were anointed to fight the Philistines, the latter's lone victory against Goliath caused all Israel to rally behind him (1 Samuel 17:51-52), while Samson's multiple victories against the same Philistines went unnoticed! Why? Because Samson was a pioneer—one who *began* the process, and one who had to deal with a greater magnitude of inertia and resistance to change.

It bears repeating: notwithstanding his individual brilliance and his record number of victories against the enemy Philistines, not one person in Israel bought into the change Samson wanted to bring. Samson's story helps us see that no matter how beautiful, timely or compelling the vision, when it comes to implementing change, inertia is the first obstacle that leaders must tackle. Which brings us to the question: how exactly can leaders tackle inertia and the complacency it brings? That question can only be answered by first taking an in-depth look at complacency—the overt evidence of inertia.

The Case of Smith, Kline and French (Even Smart People Can Become Complacent)

In the eighties, researchers at Smith, Kline and French (SKF), then one of the world's leading drug companies, developed the first H-2 receptor antagonist, a new medicine to treat ulcers. Because stomach ulcers are a very common complaint in our modern 'pressure cooker' world, SKF was smiling to the bank and making hundreds of millions of dollars annually. In the middle of that success, one of the researchers responsible for developing that medicine wrote a proposal to top management about a new line of research to develop even better medicines for treating ulcers. Top management, flush with success from the sale of the H-2 receptor antagonist, showed little interest. The researcher was forced to move to a small and unknown drug company in Sweden to work on his idea. Many years later, the small and unsung Swedish drug company unveiled a new and better class of medicines for treating ulcers—the Proton Pump Inhibitors. That unfancied Swedish company went on to make billions of dollars in the nineties. This case study reveals that even smart people aren't immune from the corrosive damage that complacency can inflict. It also shows that complacency is often the product of success.

Complacency is such a huge obstacle to change that the writer of Zephaniah has this to say about it,

> At that time I will search Jerusalem with lamps and punish those who are complacent like wine left on its dregs, who think, 'The Lord will do nothing, either good or bad.' Their wealth will be plundered, their houses demolished. (Zeph 1:12-13)

His words show us that,

A Lack of Hunger for Growth and Improvement is the Hallmark of Complacency

> At that time, I will search Jerusalem with lamps and punish those who are *complacent* like wine left on its dregs...

Vintners systematically improve the taste of wine by separating it from its dregs through a process that periodically decants the wine from one barrel to another. Therefore, "... wine left on its dregs," is symbolic of wine whose taste hasn't improved. In this sense, to be, "complacent like wine left on its dregs," is to lose your hunger for growth and to close the door to change and improvement. Complacency is hallmarked by a loss of urgency, an indifference to, and a lack of hunger for growth—all of which serve as disincentives to change.

Complacency is Often the Product of Past Success

> ...I will... punish those who are complacent... *Their wealth will be plundered, their houses demolished...*

Notice carefully that the complacent in this passage are wealthy property-owners. This is proof that success can breed complacency—the so called success trap. Harvard professor John Kotter, in his book, *A Sense of Urgency*, confirms this line of thinking, saying,

> Very, very smart people can be astonishingly complacent in the face of needed change. There are many reasons, and none more important than historical success. With sufficient success, the threats from outside are, or once were, conquered. With no need

Identify and Remove the Obstacles that Hinder Change

to focus outward, eyes shift inward to manage a larger and larger organization. Competitive instincts can also easily turn inward, creating bureaucratic politics. As a result, new problems or opportunities in the outside world are not seen clearly, if at all. Complacency grows, leading to even less interest in or focus on outside reality, leading to still more complacency.

Complacency Means You Lose the Ability to Compete

> . . . I will punish those who are complacent. . . Their wealth will be *plundered*, their houses *demolished*. . .

The word 'plunder' paints a picture of the aftermath of warfare; a time when a victorious army forcibly seizes the property and wealth of the defeated army. In competitive win-lose situations, complacency is often the first step to loss and defeat. Why? Because complacency blinds people from seeing the threats and actual strengths that newer competitors or market-players pose. No matter how far you've gone down the path of success, being complacent opens you to defeat—the case study of Smith, Kline and French proves this so well.

Complacency is a Mindset—a Way of Thinking

> . . . I . . . will punish *those who are complacent. . . who think,* "The Lord will do nothing, either good or bad.

Complacency is first and foremost an attitude, a mindset or a way of thinking. People who are complacent are distinguished by their way of thinking: they think that God isn't a factor in their affairs and what mattered yesterday will also matter tomorrow, In effect, tomorrow will be like today and nothing will ever change. If I think that what matters today is all that's going to matter tomorrow, and if I think I've mastered all that matters today, then it's no surprise if I'm laid back and complacent.

Complacency Can Be Difficult to Detect

> At that time, I will *search* Jerusalem with lamps and punish those who are complacent. . .

Did you notice that God had to put on his headlamps or searchlights before even he could spot complacency? Complacency, because it was productive yesterday, is difficult to spot today. I mean, it's hard to accuse a go-getting person who has plenty of material resources by reason of yesterday's accomplishments of complacency. To spot complacency, you'd have to look beyond material results and look at the mindset of the individual—a thing that's alien to us when it comes to dealing with supposedly successful persons. The writer of Proverbs shows us just how to detect and combat complacency, saying,

> A sluggard buries his hand in the dish; he will not even bring it back to his mouth! (Prov 19:24)

Waste is the Tell-Tale Sign of Complacency

The "sluggard" in this passage isn't poor. On the contrary, because he has his hands buried in a bowl of food, he must have been a resourceful person at some earlier stage of life. The problem at this time is that the sluggard has become complacent—unwilling to eat the food in his bowl and allowing his resources to go to waste. Therefore, waste—of money, materiel, human resources and time—and its accompanying inefficiencies are the telltale signs of complacency. Therefore, we can say that,

Combating Complacency Require that Leaders Eliminate Waste

While the chief evidence of inertia is often an insidious complacency, the telltale sign of the latter is wastefulness. Therefore combating complacency begins with doing resource audits, with checking how efficiently you and your team are using the resources of time, money and materials. While it's often easy to spot inefficient users of materials, it's more difficult to spot time wasting. How do I mean? People who don't want to be seen as complacent often put on a show of false urgency—an urgency that scurries around doing the wrong things. Leaders need to put on their searchlights and answer the questions, "Does what we (or anyone else) are doing contribute to the implementation of our proposed change?" And, "Are we doing enough of what we need to do today to bring change to pass tomorrow?"

Identify and Remove the Obstacles that Hinder Change

Wrap Around

The implementation of most types of change always requires sustained action from a group of persons. But, because people have a natural disinclination to change, effective change agents know that one of their major tasks is to remove the natural disincentives that crop up as people travel down the road of change. Parsing through organizational policies to see which one can prevent people from changing is one way to remove the factors that prevent people from changing. Another way is to look at the factors that cause inertia. The latter, and its principal symptom, complacency, are often the first obstacles that you must tackle. Tackling complacency always demands that you sniff out and cut out wastefulness. For Smith, Kline and French, the company that produced the new class of medicines for treating ulcers in the eighties; waste could have been immediately spotted in their financial statement. How? Waste could have been seen in the decreased ratio of dollars spent on research compared to dollars from sales. The huge revenue increase caused by increased sales of the new medicine wouldn't have been immediately accompanied by a corresponding increase in dollars spent on research. Long before top management refused to fund research for a newer ulcer medicine, the reduced spending on research was a telltale and objective sign that the company had become complacent. To drive change forward, leaders must first drive out inertia and complacency, and to drive out complacency, they must put an end to every kind of waste.

9

Provide Incentives to Help People Change

LEADERS WHO SUCCESSFULLY NAVIGATE change,

- Provide incentives to their people to help them make the change
- Know that incentives give people the "drive" they need to succeed.
- Know that implementing change is more an emotional/psychological thing than a logical thing
- The most compelling vision for change is one that places people at its center.

He who has a why to live can bear almost any how.

—FRIEDRICH NIETZSCHE

IMPLEMENTING CHANGE IS AKIN to going on a long march or beginning an arduous journey on a road full of obstacles, stumbling blocks and uncertainty—certainly not a task for faint minds. The people most likely to complete (or even start) the long march are those who, in the first place, know why they are on that road. Knowing "why" supplies the incentive to start and stick with the long march. Incentives supply the 'why'. They are like fuel to a fire; they empower people and give them the energy to actually go through with the change. They also help them stay the course, suffer reverses and surmount the inevitable failures and obstacles that line the road to successfully implementing change. Without the right incentives, most people wouldn't even begin to put in the effort required to turn any kind of intention into reality. And, if they do begin, then their effort wouldn't last long enough to see change become reality.

But, and this is crucial, all incentives are not born equal. The most powerful incentives are intrinsic, the kind which taps into people's innate desires for change and improvement. A less powerful, but still effective, kind of incentive are extrinsic incentives, which are based on the prospect of external rewards like money, recognition etc. Interestingly, the words of the writer of Deuteronomy, using the symbolism of a mother eagle helping her eaglets make the transition to adulthood and learn to fly, corroborate this line of thinking,

> As an eagle stirs up its nest, Hovers over its young, Spreading out its wings, taking them up, Carrying them on its wings, So the Lord alone led him, And there was no foreign god with him. (Deut 32:11-12, NKJV)

Much reflection on these words has helped me see the following truths,

Implementing Change Continues With Providing People with Intrinsic Incentives

> As an eagle... Hovers over its young, Spreading out its wings, taking them up...

Why did the fledglings (who couldn't fly) willingly hop on momma eagle's back? Why did they *choose* to go through with the novel, never-before-experienced flying lessons? Easy answer. It's because they are eaglets, and eaglets are hardwired to want to learn to fly! The change wasn't successful just because it was necessary or relevant. It was successful because it tapped into the *innate* desire of the eaglets to grow and become independent eagles. When implementing change, leaders would do well to always keep in mind the full import of these words of the writer of Deuteronomy: implementing change comes easiest when the proposed change taps into the deepest desires and aspirations of the people you influence, whether they are constituents or customers. Incentives that tap into people's innate desires are *intrinsic*—they motivate and push people to give their all without the need for external rewards like money, fame or professional recognition.

PART 3 : THE PRACTICE OF CHANGE

Implementing Change is more a Psychological thing than a Logical Thing

If, as we've seen from the case of momma eagle and her fledglings, the change that's easiest to implement is one that taps into people's innate desires, then it follows that, *implementing change is more a psychological thing than a logical thing*. Why? Because tapping into people's deepest desires and aspirations requires that leaders touch people's hearts, and not just their heads. Touching hearts is psychological and emotional; touching heads is logical. Harvard professor John Kotter drives this truth home, saying,

> People change what they do less because they are given *analysis* that shifts their *thinking* than because they are *shown* a truth that influenced their *feelings*. (Emphases in the original)

Which is why vision—the primary tool leaders use to communicate the change they'd like to bring to their groups—must resonate with the deepest needs and desires of people before change can be successfully implemented.

INCENTIVES PROVIDE PEOPLE WITH THE 'DRIVE' THEY NEED TO IMPLEMENT CHANGE

The question now becomes: why are incentives so crucial to implementing change? As I reviewed Harvard neuroscientist Gregory Bern's interesting book, *Iconoclast: A Neuroscientist Reveals How to Think Differently*, I stumbled on the following passage

> ... it is helpful to divide attention into two broad categories based on how long the process operates... *sustained attention*, as the name suggests, acts over extended periods of time and is closely related to drive and motivation... *Selective attention* is transient and detail oriented. (Emphases mine)

Professor Bern's words helped me see that incentives are powerful because they can provide people with the drive—sustained attention—they need to implement change. Because a vision of change hardly ever becomes reality without some group of persons having to work for, "extended periods of time," and because people are hardly able to work for extended periods of time without "sustained attention," providing the right incentives to constituents is critical. Incentives provide the "drive" or "motivation" that push people to give their all, not just for long periods, but also in the face of unfavorable circumstances. Therefore, we can say that implementing change requires that some persons give their all for extended periods of time, but giving your all to a cause requires that you have a reason to act—which is where incentives come in. All this agrees with the words of the writer of Proverbs,

> The laborer's appetite *works* for him; his hunger *drives* him on. (Proverbs 16:26)

Drive is Intrinsic Motivation that Helps You Give Sustained Attention to a Task

> ... *his hunger drives him on.*

The key takeaway here is that having "drive" helps you go the whole distance. Many people need to be pushed and pulled before they get the job done. With this kind of persons, the motivation to begin, continue and complete a task must necessarily be external (the so called extrinsic incentives). But, by saying,

> ... *his hunger drives him on,*

the *writer* of Proverbs helps us see that it's a force within or inside the laborer (his hunger) that's pushing or impelling him to begin, continue and complete a work task. Therefore, *drive is often revealed as a long-acting and sustained desire to make progress in a work-related area.* But the writer of Proverbs isn't through with helping us understand just what drive does. He goes on to show another critical advantage that drive gives to its possessors, saying,

> He who is full loathes honey, but to the *hungry* even what is bitter tastes sweet. (Prov 27:7)

Drive Helps You Overcome Obstacles and Setbacks

> ... *to the hungry, even what is bitter tastes sweet.*

The long road to implementing change is strewn with bitter disappointments which must be swallowed, with losses which must be absorbed, and with delays which must be endured. Drive equips its bearer with the perseverance and fortitude to go through a bitter setback and still think it sweet. In effect, people with intrinsic motivation are more likely to see a change initiative to its logical conclusion.

Further study of the words of the writer of Deuteronomy shows that momma eagle actually provided two different kinds of incentives to her fledglings before they agreed to make the change. The first, as we've seen, was intrinsic—one which tapped into their innate desires to become eagles. The second is revealed by looking again at his words,

> As an eagle stirs up its nest, Hovers over its young, Spreading out its wings, taking them up, Carrying them on its wings, So the Lord alone led him... (Deut 32:11-12, NKJV)

Implementing Change Requires that You Also Provide Extrinsic Incentives to People

> As an eagle... Spreading out its wings, taking them up, *Carrying them on its wings...*

Eagle flying school is an interesting school. Momma eagle often began flying lessons by carrying her fledglings on her wings, then, on reaching an appropriate height, she would let them fall off! The frightened fledgling, on falling off momma's back, flapped its wings furiously to keep from falling to the ground. Just before the fledgling hit the ground, momma would swoop low and put him back on her wings. By repeating this process again and again, the eaglet learned to flap its own wings and fly. In other words, eagle flying school is a process that uses repeated small quick wins to help the fledglings learn to fly. The series of small wins that the fledglings experience provides them with the incentive—in this case, extrinsic incentive—to keep at the task. Therefore, we can say that...

Implementing Change Requires the Use of Both Intrinsic and Extrinsic Incentives

Rightly divided, the words of the writer of Deuteronomy tell us that implementing change requires the use of both intrinsic and extrinsic incentives. The former taps into the innate desires of people, while the latter motivates them by providing external goals and milestones to be accomplished.

Provide Incentives to Help People Change

Intrinsic incentives are often activated by the inspirational tools of leadership—casting a clear and compelling vision, showing genuine care for people etc. In contrast, extrinsic incentives often arise from the more down-to-earth or hands-on tools of leadership—generating small quick wins, removing obstacles to change, using deadlines to combat complacency etc. Although both kinds of incentives can imbue people with the drive and enthusiasm needed to successfully implement change, the fact is that intrinsic incentives are more effective. Since the latter are often the product of a compelling and well communicated vision, it's to the subject of vision that we now turn our attention.

THE INGREDIENTS OF A COMPELLING VISION

> People are more favorable to a communication
> if they're favorable to the communicator.
>
> —Robert Cialdini

No doubt about it, drive (push or motivation), in a group setting, comes when a leader's vision for change resonates with the deepest desires of group members. A compelling and well communicated vision—one always kept in view of the right persons—is probably the most important leadership tool for imbuing people with the needed intrinsic incentives for change. Because leaders lead a great many organizations with a bewildering array of needs, it's nigh impossible to craft a generic one-size-fits-all vision statement, so the question becomes, "What exactly are the ingredients of a compelling vision?" Or, in plain terms, what are the ingredients of a vision that, when communicated, can make people more receptive to change? The writer of Proverbs, in an alternating triad of verses, provides some answers to that weighty question, saying,

> A servant will not be corrected by mere words; though he understands, he will not respond. (Prov 29:19, NKJV)

Part 3 : The Practice of Change

Leaders Who Operate only from the Premise of Positional Authority and Expertise Find it Hard to Help Others Change

> *A servant will not be corrected* by mere words...

There it is in black and white: people who are treated like "servants" are refractory to correction. And since a key fruit of correction is change, they are also refractory to change, no matter how beautifully worded the leader's vision of change is. Even though these "servants" understand what their leader is trying to get across, they still refuse to respond. In effect, leaders who depend *only* on positional power ("I am the boss!"), or expert power ("I know the subject matter"), tend to have a hard time helping people change. Indeed, their attempts to initiate change often lead to resentment and rebellion from the associates they treat as "servants." But the writer of Proverbs isn't done yet with his discourse on implementing change, he goes on to say that,

> Correct your son, and he will give you rest; Yes, he will bring delight to your soul. (Prov 29:17, NKJV)

When it Comes to Change, It's Always the Relationship Before the Facts

> Correct your *son*... *and he will give delight to your soul.*

Here we see the leader successfully correct an associate. And why did the correction process succeed? You guessed right! It was because the leader was dealing with a "son," not a "servant." As everyone knows, "sons" are always better treated and cared for than "servants" in a family setting. This means that when it comes to correcting people or communicating a vision of change, it's always the relationship *before* the facts. Why? Because people are hardwired to see truth and information through the prism of their relationship with the person communicating with them. Inexperienced leaders tend to put the cart before the horse, and think that fact or position is more important than relationship; they forget the words of psychologist Robert Cialdini,

> People are more favorable to a communication if they're favorable to the communicator.

Provide Incentives to Help People Change

When the leader is seen as distant, disrespectful and disinterested then, even if the associates understand the change she's communicating, they will not respond positively!

The writer of Proverbs drives home these truths with the third leg of his triad of verses, saying,

> He who pampers his servant from childhood will have him as a son in the end. (Prov 29:21, NKJV)

The Change Process Begins Long before the Vision for Change is Communicated!

If "servants" are refractory to correction and change, and if "sons" are "responsive" to both, then it follows that the way you treat a person long before the person needs correction matters. If you shower a "servant" with care early enough ("from childhood"), then you'll have him as a "son" ("in the end") who will willingly accept correction and be open to change. If you haven't taken the time and made the effort to develop healthy relationships with the people you lead or influence, then, no matter the relevance and beauty of your vision for change, your attempts to implement change may just hit a brick wall. Certainly, expertise, know-how and positional authority are important to the change process but, and this is crucial, historical and ongoing healthy relationships with key persons are even more important.

Correcting people is an art. Knowing who to correct—and when and how to correct—is often a litmus test of leadership. It's also the litmus test of a person's ability to kick start and continue change in a group setting. Why? Because, when accepted, correction always leads to a change in behavior. And a long-term change in behavior is critical to any kind of change that individuals or groups must make. But the ability to correct people and help them change their current behaviors is hugely dependent on the quality and history of your relationship with them. Inexperienced leaders tend to think that the major ingredient in a vision for change is expertise, leaders used to wielding the power of office tend to think that it's the position they now occupy, but effective leaders know that it's relationship, relationship, relationship. The most compelling visions for change—the ones that provide the greatest intrinsic incentives to people—are not distinguished by their beautiful content or the expertise of the communicator, but by whether they are communicated by leaders who have healthy prior relationships with their people.

Wrap Around

Implementing change is like taking people on a long march down a road strewn with obstacles and problems. Incentives provide people with the 'why', with the motivation to both begin and complete the march. They do this by giving people the 'drive' needed to give sustained attention to the task even in the face of inevitable setbacks. The best incentives are intrinsic—the kind that appeals to people's deepest longings and aspirations. Intrinsic incentives are often the product of a compelling vision communicated by experts. They are more than just beautifully worded statements of purpose; they are also pictures of a future that put people right, front and center. Why? Because the best incentives are provided by visions that clearly benefit the people to whom the vision is being communicated. And, one way to know if someone cares about you is to look at what she's done for you in the past. People don't care how much you know until they know how much you care.

10

Generate a Series of Small Wins

LEADERS WHO SUCCESSFULLY IMPLEMENT change,

- Help their people experience small wins along the way.
- know that, not experiencing any wins—big or small—for extended periods of time can doom the change process.
- know that generating small wins requires that they make the transition from producer to leader.
- know that generating small wins requires that they understand the difference between "Maker's schedule," and "Manager's schedule."
- know that generating small wins requires proactivity.

Most people won't go on the long march unless they see compelling evidence within six to eighteen months that the journey is producing expected results. Without short-term wins, too many employees give up
or actively join the resistance.

—JOHN KOTTER

THE SUCCESSFUL IMPLEMENTATION OF change of any kind often requires that people give sustained attention to a task and alter their behaviors for long periods of time—tough things to do for most of us. Therefore, intermittently along the way, people need to see compelling evidence that the road they are on is the right one, that the change they're undertaking is

PART 3 : THE PRACTICE OF CHANGE

viable, and that, in the end, they'll taste the grapes of success. Small wins provide that kind of evidence. When they come early in the journey, they are proof that the road taken is the right one, and when they occur in the middle of, or late in, the game, they give people the power to stick with their current actions and overcome hurdles. *Small wins are probably a leader's most important tool for implementing change because they are simultaneously a source of extrinsic motivation for believers, and powerful tools for convincing doubting Thomases, fence-sitters and critics.* No wonder Eric Geiger and Kevin Peck, in their book, *Designed to Lead: The Church and Leadership Development,* said that,

> Quick successes reassure the believers, convince the doubters, and confound the critics.

The writer of Deuteronomy, using the symbolism of how eaglets make the change from fledgling to adulthood, agrees with that line of thinking, saying,

> As an eagle stirs up its nest, Hovers over its young, Spreading out its wings, taking them up, Carrying them on its wings, So the LORD alone led him, And there was no foreign god with him. (Deut 32:11-12, NKJV)

His words also mean that,

Implementing Change Comes Easiest to Leaders Who Help their People Experience Small Wins Along the Way

> . . . *Spreading out its wings, taking them up, Carrying them on its wings.* . .

For the eaglets, the change from fledgling to adult is signaled by the ability to fly. And flying must be learned. But learning to fly doesn't occur in one fell swoop. It happens through a series of small wins as momma eagle, "[Carries] them on her wings," and soars into the sky, before deliberately letting them fall off. It's the flapping of those wings which occurs when the eaglets intermittently fall off momma's back that strengthens the fledglings and slowly helps them learn to fly. In essence, change for the eaglets comes via a series of small wins. The best change agents are those who take this truth to heart: *implementing change comes easiest to leaders who help their people experience small wins along the way.* And not experiencing

Generate a Series of Small Wins

any success—big or small—for extended periods of time can doom the implementation process. The words of the writer of Zechariah show just why all this is so. The latter records the discouragement and challenges that Jewish returnees from Babylonian exile had to face as they began the long and arduous task of rebuilding the temple at Jerusalem under the leadership of a man called Zerubbabel.

> The hands of Zerubbabel have laid the foundation of this temple; His hands shall also finish it. Then you will know that the LORD of hosts has sent me to you. *For who has despised the day of small things?* For these seven rejoice to see the plumb line in the hand of Zerubbabel. They are the eyes of the LORD, Which scan to and fro throughout the whole earth. (Zech 4:9-10, NKJV)

These wise words show us that, when it comes to implementing change,

Small Wins Are Often Despised By People in Authority, but Valued By those Without It

> *... For who has despised the day of small things?"*

The answer to that weighty question is, "Leaders and people in authority!" And here's why. It's because leaders are people who, from the get-go, naturally "own" the vision and are in a position to always see the big picture. They therefore have little need to experience a steady stream of small wins to keep them going along the rough road to implementing change. Not so for associates and followers who normally don't "own" the vision. Small wins are of great value to this group of persons because they provide visible proof that the road they are on is the right road. In effect, leaders are encouraged by vision, while followers are encouraged by results. *When it comes to implementing change, the best leaders know that there's a dichotomy between leaders and followers. The latter need to experience small wins to help them stay the course, while the former are often majorly encouraged by their vision for change.* Academics Chip and Dan Heath underscore the point, saying,

> One way to motivate action, then, is to make people feel as though they're already closer to the finish line than they might have thought.

PART 3 : THE PRACTICE OF CHANGE

The people who most need this kind of motivating are the people in the trenches, and one way to make them,

> feel as though they're already closer to the finish line than they might have thought,

is to generate quick and regular small wins.

Small Wins Work because they Reduce the Perceived Amount of Effort and Skill Needed to Implement Change

> ... For who has despised *the day of small things?* For... [They]... shall see *the plumb line in the hand of Zerubbabel.* ..

Did you notice that the day of small things is associated with the use of a plumb line? The plumb line is a piece of string with a bob of heavy metal at the end used to measure the height and straightness of completed walls. Since the walls of the temple were many, the completion of each wall was essentially a small win. But, and this is crucial, each wall was declared finished and true to plumb only after it was measured with a plumb line. In effect, the plumb line symbolically refers to the simplicity and reduced skill levels required to generate each small win, and the sense of satisfaction that that gives to workers. Again, Chip and Dan Heath, drive the point home, saying,

> Psychologist Karl Weick, in a paper, *Small Wins: Redefining the Scale of Social Problems,* said, A small win reduces importance ('this is no big deal'), reduces demands ('that's all that needs to be done'), and raises perceived skill levels ('I can do at least that').

All three of these factors will tend to make change easier and more self-sustaining."

Small Wins Generate Momentum

Every time you generate a small win, your vision for change "speaks," causing more people to join the bandwagon, and even more to continue with the actions they've already started. As a result, the whole process gains momentum and becomes easier to steer as more resources (finances, people etc.) come on board. Author and entrepreneur Scott Belsky puts it beautifully, saying,

Generate a Series of Small Wins

As a human being, you are motivated by progress. When you see concrete evidence of progress, you are more inclined to take further action.

Small wins are the, "concrete evidence of progress," which help motivate more persons to, "take further action"—actions that make successful change both easier and more likely. All this leads to the next question: how exactly can leaders generate the quick small wins they need to successfully drive change? Further study of Scripture has helped me see that generating small wins requires,

1. Leaders who make the transition from 'producer' to 'leader',
2. Leaders who understand the difference between 'Maker's schedule' and 'Manager's schedule' and,
3. Leaders who are always proactive.

TO CONSISTENTLY GENERATE SMALL WINS, CHANGE AGENTS MUST MAKE THE TRANSITION FROM 'PRODUCER' TO 'LEADER'

Good leaders make things happen. They get results... Not only are they productive individually, but they also are able to help the team produce.

—JOHN MAXWELL.

Recently, as part of a new strategy to defeat the Boko Haram-led insurgency in northeastern Nigeria, Nigeria's newly elected president directed the chief of army staff to relocate from the capital city Abuja to the city of Maiduguri, the epicenter of the insurgency. To a student of leadership, that directive is intriguing because it automatically raises the following questions: is the army chief taking over the job of the field commanders in the zone of conflict? What happens if some other insurgency breaks out in another part of the country, will the chief of staff be in two or more places simultaneously? What now happens to the original duties of the chief of army staff? *More importantly, the directive unearths the age-old question of whether leaders should do the job themselves or get the job done through others.* Interestingly, the writer of Proverbs weighs in on the matter, saying,

PART 3 : THE PRACTICE OF CHANGE

> An employer who hires a fool or a bystander is like an archer who shoots recklessly. (Prov 26:10, NLT)

These words mean that

Leaders Are People Who Get Results Through Others

This illuminating passage of Scripture likens leaders ("employers") to archers who miss the mark and are unable to hit their targets because they employed the wrong persons ("bystanders and fools"). In effect, a leader is one whose productivity is, in part, determined by others; one whose ability to hit the target is influenced by the quality of her hires, associates or partners. If you're a leader, you're dependent on others to get the job done. Or as management teacher Stephen Covey puts it,

> Any time you step from independence [I can do it alone] to interdependence [I choose to do the job with or through you], you step into leadership.

This means that. . .

Effective Leaders Get Results through Others without Necessarily Taking over their Jobs

The best leaders do more than just get results in their own personal lives; they go one step further and get results through others *without taking over their jobs*. Probably the most difficult leadership transition to make is to move from primary producer or doer (the one who does the job) to leader (one who enables others do their own jobs). I mean, who hasn't heard about the productive shop floor staff whose results got him promoted to shop floor manager and who, to the chagrin of all, failed at his new job. The productive shop floor staff failed to make the transition from producer to leader. To Israel's hurt, Shamgar, one of Israel's least known and most talented leaders, failed to make that kind of transition. The writer of Judges narrates Shamgar's eye-opening story. . .

> After him was Shamgar the son of Anath, who killed six hundred men of the Philistines with an ox goad; and he also delivered [led] Israel. (Judg 3:31, NKJV)

Shamgar was a Superb Individual Producer

No doubt about it, Shamgar was another Samson—a gifted soldier who could annihilate an entire battalion of enemy Philistine soldiers while armed with nothing but an ox-goad! But being an individual producer is hugely different from being a leader or manager. How do I mean? Listen again to the writer of Judges as he gives an account of the leadership of Shamgar,

> In the days of Shamgar, son of Anath. . . The highways were deserted, And the travelers walked along the byways. Village life ceased, it ceased in Israel, Until I, Deborah, arose, Arose a mother in Israel. . . Then there was war in the gates; Not a shield or spear was seen among forty thousand in Israel. (Judges 5:6-8, NKJV)

Shamgar's Leadership was a Sham Because He Didn't Make the Transition from Producer to Leader

> In the days of Shamgar. . . *the highways were deserted, travellers walked in byways. Village life ceased. . .*

Imagine living in a country where the security situation is so bad, people can't lead normal lives—

> Village life ceased,

—and traveling from one place to another is fraught with danger:

> the highways were deserted, travellers walked in byways,

simply because criminals are doing their thing. These grim words of the writer of Judges help us see that, although Shamgar was a great individual producer who could vanquish a battalion of enemy soldiers alone, his appointment as Judge of Israel and leader of the army actually made Israel an insecure place! The question becomes, "Why did such a productive individual producer fail when appointed as leader of men?" The answers to that important question lie hidden in the words of the writer of Judges. Those words show that,

Part 3 : The Practice of Change

People Who Make the Transition from Producer to Leader Always Bear in Mind that their Main Job is to Help Others Do their Own Jobs

Why was,

> ...not a shield or spear... seen among forty thousand in Israel?

Or, in simple terms, why was the army not equipped or provided with the weapons she needed to get the job done? It's because Shamgar, by reason of his unusual skill at soldiering, decided to do the job of the army all by himself! I mean, why bother to call out the troops when you can do it all by yourself? And, if you can, by yourself, kill off all the enemy troops, why bother to equip the troops? Shamgar's case reveals an all too common mistake that first class individual producers often make—they attempt to do the jobs of followers rather than help followers do their own jobs. Writer Scott Belsky, in his book, *Making Ideas Happen,* said that,

> The first symptom of an inability to scale [build an organization] is finding yourself doing things that can be done by others (although, admittedly not quite as well). Yes, it is always ideal when the head designer, the company founder, or the architect with her or his name on the door can deal directly with any inquiry. However, in taking on such a task, the leader is not doing the things that only he/she can do. Leaders of any creative endeavor should focus first on the things that only they can do—things that simply couldn't be delegated to others.

When you find yourself, like Shamgar, doing what someone else in your organization can do, you're not scaling up and you probably wouldn't get the small wins you need to drive change. Why? Because *small wins come when people are empowered to do their own jobs, not when you do everything yourself.*

Leaders Who Get Results through Others are 'Providers'

> In the days of Shamgar... *not a shield or spear was seen among forty thousand in Israel...*

Shamgar didn't succeed as a leader because, not only did he do the job of the army, he also didn't provide the latter with the resources (shields, spears and weapons) they needed to do their own job. Making the transition from

Generate a Series of Small Wins

producer to manager requires that your priority becomes providing the resources—tools, training etc—for others to do their own jobs. You must consciously avoid doing the job yourself. If someone can't get the job done, then you can either re-train or replace them.

Leaders Who Get Results through Others are 'Enablers'

> In the days of Shamgar... *war came to the city gates...*

In ancient Israel, the city gate was a place where the leading men and women sat to adjudicate disputes and ratify agreements—much like our modern day court system. Tellingly, under Shamgar's leadership,

> ...war came to the city gates...

In other words, disputes went unresolved and even degenerated into open and violent conflict. Shamgar was so concerned with *doing*, with carrying out the task alone, that he left unattended the more important task of *enabling*, of ensuring that the team's conflicts were smoothly settled, of casting vision and keeping the team's mission right, front and center of everyone. Shamgar couldn't manage the team. Leaders who generate short-term wins must work through others; they must be willing to invest a great deal of their time and effort in maintaining team harmony and cohesion—things which create the conditions that allow others make a contribution.

What does all this mean for change agents? It means that they must fight off the temptation to do the job themselves. Just because you can do it doesn't mean you *should* do it. That temptation feeds your ego but builds weakness into your organization and makes it hard to generate small wins—the results—you need to drive the change process.

LEADERS WHO CONSISTENTLY GENERATE SMALL WINS KNOW THE DIFFERENCE BETWEEN 'MAKER'S SCHEDULE' AND 'MANAGER'S SCHEDULE'

> *Teach us to number our days*, that we may gain a heart of wisdom. (Psalm 90:12)

This intriguing passage of Scripture asserts that,

> ... [numbering] *our days*,

PART 3 : THE PRACTICE OF CHANGE

—measuring time, knowing how long it takes to complete an assignment etc—can provide us wisdom and insight into process. Numerous studies have confirmed the thinking of the Psalmist, but probably the most insightful has been that of Paul Graham, founder of the venture capital firm, Y-Combinator. In his eye-opening paper, *Maker's Schedule, Manager's Schedule*, Paul Graham asserts that understanding how the time use pattern of producers is significantly different from that of managers is critical to leading a team. He went on to say that...

> There are two types of schedule, which I'll call the manager's schedule and the maker's schedule. The manager's schedule is for bosses. It's embodied in the traditional appointment book, with each day cut into one hour intervals. You can block off several hours for a single task if you need to, but by default you change what you're doing every hour. When you use time that way, it's merely a practical problem to meet with someone. Find an open slot in your schedule, book them, and you're done. Most powerful people are on the manager's schedule. It's the schedule of command. But there's another way of using time that's common among people who make things, like programmers and writers. They generally prefer to use time in units of half a day at least. You can't write or program well in units of an hour. That's barely enough time to get started. When you're operating on the maker's schedule, meetings are a disaster. A single meeting can blow a whole afternoon, by breaking it into two pieces each too small to do anything hard in. Plus you have to remember to go to the meeting. That's no problem for someone on the manager's schedule. There's always something coming on the next hour; the only question is what. But when someone on the maker's schedule has a meeting, they have to think about it.

In effect, leaders who don't understand these two very different schedules can demand that the producers who work under them run a 'manager's schedule', hobbling their people's ability to produce the necessary short-term wins. *The people who make the transition from producer to leader hold meetings and demand accountability at times that don't impinge on the ability of their producers to produce.* What does all this mean for change agents? It means that they must be acutely aware of the quantity of time, quality of time and times of the day that the producers under them need to generate results. And, this is crucial, they must then adapt their own schedules to those of their producers.

Generate a Series of Small Wins

LEADERS WHO CONSISTENTLY GENERATE SMALL WINS ARE ALWAYS PROACTIVE

The more concerned you become with things you can't control, the less you will do to improve the things you can control.

—John Maxwell

Management writer Stephen Covey, in his landmark book, *The Seven Habits of Highly Effective People,* introduced the concepts of the circle of influence and the circle of concern. He went on to argue that the former contains all the things within our power—what schools my children attend, whether I exercise today or not, what books I read etc. In contrast, the circle of concern includes things like Russia's influence on the Syrian civil war, the Israeli-Palestinian Conflict etc., things over which I have little or no control. Dr. Covey insists that effective leaders concentrate their actions on the things they can control—things in their circle of influence—and spend less time in their circle of concern. Interestingly, the writer of Proverbs agrees with him, saying,

> Sensible people keep their eyes glued on wisdom, but a fool's eyes wander to the ends of the earth. (Prov 17:24, NLT)

Proactivity Chooses to focus on the Things it Can Control—on Things Within its Power

Effectiveness always begins when leaders *choose* to,

> keep their eyes glued on wisdom [in this sense, what's right in front of them],

(in their circle of influence), and cease being fixated on things at,

> . . . the ends of the earth.

(in their circle of concern). In simple terms, the best leaders are proactive; consciously choosing to act only on matters over which they have some degree of influence. Every time I'm tempted to worry about something, I settle the issue by asking myself these questions: is the matter within my control? Is there something—no matter how small—that I can do to influence the situation? Will my intervention make a difference? Proactivity generates quick small wins because it encourages leaders to take charge and concentrate their resources on the areas over which they have some influence. Leaders who are inordinately fixated on the things they cannot control, on the things in their circle of concern, become passive and reactive—doing less than they should about the things they can actually control.

Proactivity has Two Opposites—Passivity and 'Reactivity'

Proactivity has two opposites—passivity, which chooses to do nothing or to stop doing something, and "reactivity," which chooses to do the wrong or irresponsible thing because it's fixated on the fact that all it needs to succeed is not now within its control. Passivity and reactivity, because they choose to focus on their circles of concern, breed frustration, paralyzing worry and hopelessness. When you focus on what you don't now have or on issues over which you have little or no control, you begin to develop a sense of despondency, disillusionment, disempowerment and despair—what I call the 4Ds of defeat. In contrast, *proactivity says, "How can I use what I now possess wisely? While passivity says, "Of what value is the little that I have today?"* The difference—the quick small wins generated—is not in the resources but in the decisions!

Wrap Around

Implementing change is like taking a long march along a road running through hostile territory, and strewn with hardship and setbacks. This makes it mandatory for leaders to give their people proof that the road they're taking is the right one. Small wins—a series of quick results along the road—are visible proof that the road people are on is the right one. The best change agents know that while leaders and persons in authority may be encouraged by a vision of change, followers and associates are encouraged by the results that small wins offer. Generating small wins requires leaders who are willing to make the transition from producer to leader, from a person who does it all by herself to one who does it through and with others. Helping people generate frequent small wins requires that you help them focus on the things within their control. Working on the things within their control makes them more effective and more likely to generate small wins.

Generate a Series of Small Wins

Whatever, the best change agents always keep this truth in mind: not generating any small win for long periods of time can doom the implementation of change.

11

Cultivate a Core Team

- Change that's both successful and enduring is one that's driven by a core team, not by a lone leader.
- Core teams are high-performance teams that help generate the small wins essential to convincing everyone that they are headed in the right direction.
- Core teams help make change "sticky"—not easily reversed after you leave office or step down.

Every successful venture has a core team to make it work. Failure to nurture that team's effectiveness and loyalty will jeopardize anything that has been achieved.

—MAX MCKEOWN.

THE STORY IS THE stuff of many a Sunday school teaching: Israel had transgressed against her God, so he let them experience oppression and slavery under the Philistines for forty years [Judges 13:1]. Imagine being under military subjugation by a cruel foreign power for a whole forty years. Imagine again, the amount of work required to liberate the nation from that long period of domination and slavery. That work of liberation was the destiny and mission of Israel's one-man army, Samson. Listen to the writer of Judges,

Cultivate a Core Team

> For, lo, thou shalt conceive, and bear a son; and no razor shall come on his head: for the child [Samson]. . . *shall begin to deliver Israel out of the hand of the Philistines.* (Judg 13:5, KJV)

Not Having a Core Team Meant that Samson Could Only Begin the Work of Change

> [Samson]. . . shall *begin* to deliver Israel. . .

Samson attacked the Philistine army with deadly effect again and again. At one point, he even killed a thousand of them while armed with only the jawbone of a donkey! But there's more to the story. Over the years, as I've read and re-read his story, something consistently sticks out like a sore thumb: no matter how successful Samson was at killing and defeating the Philistines, no one—not one Israelite—ever rallied to his side! This is probably the reason Samson's herculean efforts made hardly a dent in the Philistine military structures that oversaw the subjugation of Israel. Not having a team to help with the work meant that Samson—despite his immense personal giftedness and herculean efforts—could only *begin* the work of delivering Israel! He never could carry it to *completion*.

David's Team Helped Him Complete the Task

Samson's results are in stark contrast to the work of David—who completely destroyed the Philistine army so that it never again posed a threat to Israel. David was able to get the job done because he had a team famously known as "David's mighty men," to help him. The importance of that team (which I refer to as "Team David") is revealed by the fact that, although David killed Goliath in the now-famous contest at the valley of Elah, all the other four brothers of Goliath (giants themselves) were killed by members of Team David [2 Samuel 21:19]. Symbolically, what David started was completed by other members of his team. All this shows that implementing change requires that the change agent consciously develop a core team to help push the change through. Which brings us to the question: what was the nature of Team David ("David's mighty men"), or more to the point, what kind of team is needed to implement change? The answers to those questions are revealed by a close study of the nature and composition of Team David. Listen to the writer of Second Samuel,

PART 3 : THE PRACTICE OF CHANGE

> These are the names of David's *mightiest* men. The first was Jashobeam the Hacmonite, who was commander of *the Three—the three greatest warriors among David's men*. He once used his spear to kill eight hundred enemy warriors in a single battle. *Next in rank* among the Three was Eleazar son of Dodai. *Once, Eleazar and David stood together against the Philistines when the entire Israelite army had fled.* He killed Philistines until his hand was too tired to lift his sword, and the LORD gave him a great victory that day. The rest of the army did not return until it was time to collect the plunder! *Next in rank* was Shammah son of Agee from Harar. One time the Philistines gathered at Lehi and attacked the Israelites in a field full of lentils. *The Israelite army fled, but Shammah held his ground in the middle of the field and beat back the Philistines. So the* LORD brought about a great victory. Once during harvest time, when David was at the cave of Adullam, the Philistine army was camped in the valley of Rephaim. *The Three (who were among the Thirty—an elite group among David's fighting men)* went down to meet him there. (2 Sam 23:8-13, NLT)

This amazing passage is a treasure trove of insights into the nature, inner workings, and composition of Team David. It shows that,

Team David was a Team of Teams—made Up of Concentric Groups of Persons, With an Elite High-Performance Team at its Core

> These are the names of David's *mightiest* men. The first was Jashobeam the Hacmonite, who was commander *of the Three—the three greatest warriors among David's men*...

Most people are familiar with the expression, "David's mighty men," but, by using the phrase, "David's *mightiest* men," this passage takes that expression one step further; helping us see that there was a core of soldiers within the larger group who were more skillful, more dependable, and closer to David than others. The writer of Second Samuel drives the point home, when he goes on to say,

> ... *The Three (who were among the Thirty—an elite group among David's fighting men)*...

There it is in black and white: there was an elite core of dependable high performers within the larger thirty-man-strong Team David! This elite core were the ones who often stood with David during the gravest crises, and who could be counted on to get the job done in the most difficult of times. In modern parlance, they were a high-performance team (kind of like the Navy Seals among other well trained soldiers).

Team David Was a Team of Experts

By using the term,

> ... Next in rank,

not once, but twice, the writer of Second Samuel reveals another key to the composition of Team David: it was a team of experts. Retired US Army general Stanley McCrystal, in his book, *Team of Teams*, said that,

> Rank is used to assign authority and responsibility commensurate with demonstrated ability and experience. Leaders of higher ranks are expected to possess the skills and judgment required to deploy their forces and care for their soldiers.

His words shed light on the phrase, "Next in rank"—helping us see that Team David was made up of persons whose positions or ranks were entirely merit based. But there's still more to the story of Team David. Listen once again to the writer of Second Samuel,

> Once during harvest time, when David was at the cave of Adullam, the Philistine army was camped in the valley of Rephaim. The Three (who were among the Thirty—an elite group among David's fighting men) went down to meet him there. David was staying in the stronghold at the time, and a Philistine detachment had occupied the town of Bethlehem. David remarked longingly to his men, "Oh, how I would love some of that good water from the well in Bethlehem, the one by the gate." So the Three broke through the Philistine lines, drew some water from the well, and brought it back to David. But he refused to drink it. Instead, he poured it out before the LORD. "The LORD forbid that I should drink this!" he exclaimed. "*This water is as precious as the blood of these men who risked their lives to bring it to me.*" So David did not drink it. This is an example of the exploits of the Three. (2 Sam 23:13-17, NLT)

PART 3 : THE PRACTICE OF CHANGE

Team David Was a Team of Loyalists

Imagine, David (a native of Bethlehem) voices his longing to drink, not just water, but water from the well at the gate of his hometown. His top three leaders (members of the elite high performance core) hear this longing and, putting their lives in jeopardy, break through enemy lines at the town of Bethlehem to fetch him the water he so longs for! These men were the epitome of loyalty—willing to do all and lay down their lives for their leader and his vision. Not to be outdone, David himself shows loyalty to his brave subordinates. How? By refusing to drink the water they fetched; instead he poured it out as an offering to God! Loyalty upwards (from associate to leader) is easiest where there's also loyalty downwards (from leader to associate). In the face of the gravest troubles, and when everyone had fled, it was only the members of this elite group who stood with David—

> . . . *Once during harvest time, when David was at the cave of Adullam, the Philistine army was camped in the valley of Rephaim. The Three (who were among the Thirty—an elite group among David's fighting men) went down to meet him there. . .*

Core Teams Help Make Change Sticky, Generate Small Wins, And Are Less Likely to Fall Away in Times of Trouble

Successfully implementing change always takes more than the knowledge and expertise of just one person (no matter how gifted that person is, and you can ask Samson!). It requires the coordinated efforts of a highly skilled group of persons. For David, whose mission was mainly martial (the military overthrow of the Philistine army), the skills needed to be part of the core team were majorly martial—soldiering, the command of men, and the management of violence. While the change you want to implement is unlikely to be of the military kind, the principles still apply: you need to consciously bring on board the best hands in your organization and use a merit-based ranking system to develop a dependable and loyal core that can help you get the necessary small wins even under the most unfavorable conditions. Core teams are crucial to the successful implementation of change largely because of three reasons: firstly because they make change "sticky," or difficult to reverse. As the example of Team David—who later killed all four brothers of the giant Goliath—shows, core groups can carry the can and complete the change not only when the leader is in office, but also *after she's left office*. The second reason a core group is important is that their expertise helps you more easily generate a series of short-term wins. Small quick wins are mission-critical to implementing change because they strengthen the believers, win over fence-sitters, convince the doubters and silence the naysayers. The final reason core teams are important is that, when everyone else is discouraged and has left you, members of the core team are more likely to remain. Because core teams are so crucial to implementing change, and because they must operate like high-performance teams, it's to the latter that we now turn our attention.

TURNING YOUR CORE TEAM INTO A HIGH-PERFORMANCE TEAM

A chain is as strong as its weakest link.

—THOMAS REID

Some time ago, the mentally ill co-pilot of a German airplane locked out his chief pilot from the cockpit and proceeded to fly the airplane into a mountainside—killing hundreds of passengers in the process. That distressing incident made me take another look at, and even begin to question, the popular cliché,

A chain is as strong as its weakest link.

Come to think of it, that cliché assumes that all chains should have weak links! But, as the example of the mentally disturbed co-pilot in the airplane crash described above shows, there are certain teams that can't afford to have weak links. All links in such chains must be strong. That category of teams is high-performance teams, what General Stanley McCrystal refers to as "mission critical teams." Indeed, in his book, *Team of Teams*, the general said that,

> Mission Critical Teams" (MCTs)—small teams whose failure will likely lead to loss of life, and whose time frames for action often involve critical periods of ten minutes or less.

What he refers to as MCTs, I extend and build upon, and refer to as high-performance teams (HPTs). The latter are small groups—emergency medical teams, air cabin crews, special forces soldiers etc—whose

PART 3 : THE PRACTICE OF CHANGE

performance must be excellent at all times, who operate under conditions with little room for error, and whose failure can lead to loss of life or catastrophe. In short, HPTs are teams *without weak links*—teams that must win all the time—great models for the core teams that change agents can use to implement change. Imagine my surprise when I saw the criteria for creating an HPT in, of all places, the book of Isaiah! Listen to the writer of Isaiah,

> Wail, O gate! Howl, O city! Melt away, all you Philistines! *A cloud of smoke comes from the north, and there's not a straggler in its ranks.* (Isaiah 14:31)

These amazing words show that the mighty army of the Philistines (who had militarily subjugated Israel for all of forty years) was itself going to be overwhelmed by another military force that, like a cloud of smoke, could not be withstood. They also show that,

High Performance Teams Are a Cut Above the Competition

> Wail You Philistines! *A cloud of smoke* comes from the north...

Ordinarily, smoke can permeate and penetrate any defense. Indeed, defending yourself or your position from a cloud of smoke is well-nigh impossible. The Philistine army faced just such an impossible task—fighting an enemy that was like a cloud of smoke. When you need your team to generate the small wins that help drive change, then you need to transform it into a "cloud of smoke," into the best in the business, into an HPT.

High Performance Teams Are Teams Without Weak Links

> Wail... you Philistines! A cloud of smoke comes from the north and *there is not a straggler in its ranks.*

By definition, a straggler is one who can't keep up with the rest of the team. In this sense, a straggler is a weak link. This means that what made the enemy unbeatable—like a cloud of smoke—was the fact that there were no weak links or stragglers in its ranks! High Performance Teams—the teams that are a cut above the competition—are groups without weak links in their ranks. So how can you create a team without a weak link? The writer of Isaiah helps us with an answer, saying...

Cultivate a Core Team

... A cloud of smoke comes from the north and there is not a straggler *in its ranks*. (Isaiah 14:31)

High Performance Teams Operate a Ranking System

....and there is not a straggler in its ranks.

HPTs utilize a ranking system. This system is more than just hierarchical; it's also a means to measure and reward performance. Again, General McCrystal's words on ranking re-echo,

> Rank is used to assign authority and responsibility commensurate with demonstrated ability and experience. Leaders of higher ranks are expected to possess the skills and judgment required to deploy their forces and care for their soldiers.

A ranking system should be used to objectively assess the *latest* capabilities of current and future members of your core team. This system holds people to such *high* standards that it weeds out stragglers and weak links. In simple terms, HPTs are able to deliver the goods all the time because they not only constantly use examinations and evaluations to assess, rank and reward team members; they also use them to remove weak links. Interestingly, since the crash of the German airliner (mentioned above), the German authorities have rolled out new and tighter regulations to test the mental health status of all pilots and cabin crew, and weed out the "weak links."

The successful implementation of change requires the creation of a core group of persons to drive the process. The best change agents—the ones who see their vision for change become reality—are those who, like David, set high standards for the members of their core group. But the ultimate test of a core team's strength lies in what happens when the teams senior leader isn't available for any number of reasons—retirement, sickness or removal from office. It's to that test of strength that we now turn our attention.

HOW STRONG IS YOUR CORE TEAM?

It's an all too common phenomenon: ostensibly with the approval of all, a charismatic leader with a vision for change begins to implement a change initiative. The initiative gathers momentum as results begin to flow. The people are confident that they are on the right road. Then, for a thousand and one reasons ranging from retirement, promotion to another division or even death, the leader has to leave. Her departure causes results to diminish and enthusiasm to dwindle. Soon, the change initiative is modified, neglected or, worse still, abandoned. Everything returns to square one. To help understand why that phenomenon is played out in organization after organization, we need to travel over to the realm of the physical sciences.

Engineers determine the strength of a material by measuring how much stress it can cope with before it breaks up, breaks down or breaks apart. To them, a diamond is one of the world's hardest objects because it requires huge amounts of energy to break up. So how do students of leadership measure the strength of organizations? While organizations may face a variety of stressors—financial problems, negative market conditions and political upheavals—probably the single greatest threat to a group's performance and survival is the loss of, or change in, its top-leaders (especially its CEO). Stanford professors Jeffrey Pfeffer and Robert Sutton, in their excellent book, *Hard Facts: Dangerous Half-truths and Total Nonsense*, said that,

> One study showed that Toyota was the only major automobile company where a change in CEO had no effect on performance.

Therefore, we can say that Toyota is strong because the firm's performance is little affected by the removal or change of its senior leader. Imagine my surprise when I saw these same truths writ large in the operations of Team Daniel (the team of Daniel, Hananiah, Mishael and Azariah)—young Hebrew exiles who served in the court of King Nebuchadnezzar of Babylon! Listen to the writer of Daniel,

> This made [king Nebuchadnezzar] so angry... that he ordered the execution of all the wise men of Babylon. So... men were sent to look for Daniel and his friends to put them to death. Then Daniel returned to his house and explained the matter to his friends Hananiah, Mishael, and Azariah....Then was the secret revealed to Daniel in a night vision... [Daniel said]... The great God has shown the king what will take place in the future..... *Then the king fell before Daniel* and... said... Surely your God is the God of gods... (Dan 2:12-13, 17, 45-47)

Cultivate a Core Team

Daniel's Leadership Saves His Team!

King Nebuchadnezzar was the quintessential oriental despot—capricious and cruel. In this famous passage, the king had a dream which he wanted his advisers to interpret. But, there was a catch: the king had forgotten the dream! Notwithstanding, he demanded that his advisers tell him the interpretation or meaning of the dream! The flummoxed advisers told him that that was an impossible task. Enraged, the king ordered the execution of all his advisers. This was the reason Daniel and his three friends (Team Daniel), who were royal advisers, were also going to be executed. Team Daniel faced this challenge together and with the help of God (who revealed the king's dream to Daniel), a gifted Daniel was able to provide Nebuchadnezzar with the solution he craved. The result, *"the king fell before Daniel,"* and paid him obeisance! Test taken and passed. Sometime later we see Team Daniel face another life and death challenge at the hands of, believe or not, the same King Nebuchadnezzar. For some reason, Daniel the team leader is absent when this challenge occurs. And how did the team fare in his absence? Listen again to the writer of Daniel;

> King Nebuchadnezzar made an image of gold. . . and set it up. . . whoever does not fall down and worship will immediately be thrown into a blazing furnace. . . But there are some Jews. . . who pay no attention to you, O king. . . Nebuchadnezzar commanded. . . soldiers. . . *to tie up Shedrach, Meshach and Abednego and throw them into the blazing furnace. . .* Then the king said, "Praise be to the God of Shedrach, Meshach and Abednego, who sent His angel and rescued His servants. . . (Dan 3:1-8, 12-13, 22)

Team Daniel Passes the Test—Without Daniel!

Nebuchadnezzar, cruel and capricious as ever, set up a ninety feet tall golden statue on the outskirts of his capital. He then commanded everyone assembled there to bow before the statue whenever a herald played a signature tune. People had to "face the music" or pay with their lives! While everyone chose to bow before the golden statue, the members of Team Daniel decided to disobey the king's orders. By saying,

> . . . Nebuchadnezzar commanded. . . soldiers. . . *to tie up Shedrach, Meshach and Abednego and throw them into the blazing furnace,*

the writer of Daniel helps us see that, for some reason, Daniel wasn't present at this event. In effect, without their charismatic leader Daniel, Team Daniel defied Nebuchadnezzar's orders to worship a golden idol and got thrown into a blazing furnace for their comeuppance. The question becomes: will Team Daniel be able to pass such a crucial test without its talismanic leader? The answer is: the team puts its trust in God and is delivered from the blazing furnace. Team Daniel passes the test without its leader. Notice carefully that, even though Daniel their leader was absent, the team got the exact same results they had obtained when Daniel led them. The team was strong because it passed the key test of adversity—the absence of a key leader. This brings me to my next point:

Strong Core Teams Aren't Built Around a Single Strong Leader

Strong teams—like Team Daniel— are groups that can keep obtaining results even when they lose the services of key leaders. And this is because they have strong leadership development pipelines and programs as our next case study reveals...

The Case of Akio Morita and Sony Corporation USA

Akio Morita was the charismatic chairman of Sony Corporation, USA. His genius lay in miniaturization and marketing, and he was majorly responsible for the development of the Sony Walkman and the Sony Discman—runaway bestsellers that revolutionized the market for portable music players in the eighties and nineties. It was even said that Sony introduced both products without the benefit of a market survey! Sadly, after Mr. Morita's untimely death, Sony completely ceded the market for portable music to Apple (think iPod and iTunes). In short, the death of Mr. Morita simply revealed the weakness of Sony's core team—they couldn't continue to obtain results after the death of their leader.

Wrap Around

Although a hugely gifted lone leader can often begin implementing change, the continuation and successful completion of change always requires the creation and cultivation of a core team. The latter are high performance teams that generate the small wins needed to encourage the faithful and

Cultivate a Core Team

convince the critics. Because they help complete what the senior leader starts, core teams help make change "sticky"—hard to reverse after the senior leader leaves office. The strongest core teams are those that can still run with the vision for change after the departure or removal of the leader. Core teams are also hallmarked by their unusual degree of loyalty. When everyone else is falling away by reason of challenges and unfavorable circumstances, members of the core team are the ones most likely to stick with the leader.

12

Make Change Stick (Culture Matters)

ALL TYPES OF CHANGE aren't born equal. Some changes are superficial, while others attempt to do deeper things. When change challenges the deepest and most widely shared beliefs of a group of persons by requiring them to act in new ways that oppose or negate those beliefs, then that change will come up against culture. That kind of change—the one that "challenges" the culture of a group—will likely gender unusually fierce and prolonged resistance, and is unlikely to succeed. And, if at first it does succeed, the success is often temporary because, at the first opportunity—the leader leaves office, there's a change of guards etc—the change initiative will be halted, modified, reversed or even abandoned. Therefore, making change "stick" ("sticky change" is long lasting change) often requires leaders who are culturally savvy. MIT professor Edgar Schein, in his book, *The Corporate Culture Survival Guide,* makes all this plain when he said that,

> ... if core elements of the culture need to be transformed, planned change processes may not work, leading change leaders to institute more drastic processes...

His words show that there's a connection between change and culture, and that cultural issues can serve as barriers to the implementation of change. They also show a much ignored truth: leaders who attempt to implement change may just also be stepping into a cultural minefield. Indeed, as Professor Schein's words reveal, the more fundamental the change you propose, the greater the role culture plays in determining its successful implementation. Which brings us to the question, what kind of leader is in the best position to implement change? That question is largely answered by the following case study...

The Case of the Nigerian President Who Attempted to Reform the Almajiri (Islamic) System of Education

Have you ever entered a room and become conscious of its smell and wondered why insiders who've been there longer can't seem to perceive the smell as strongly as you do? Most people have, and a few have even tried to do something about it. But knowing that the room doesn't smell too good isn't enough to change it, you also need to be careful to not offend the sensibilities of the persons in it. In other words, being a complete outsider—a person who understands little about the dynamics of the people in the room—might start, but probably never finish the job of changing the room's odor. This was the position of newly elected Nigerian president Goodluck Jonathan when his administration attempted to solve the *Almajiri* issue in northern Nigeria. The Almajiri educational system allows parents to send off tens of thousands of boys (some as young as five years), popularly referred to as Almajiri, to study under Islamic teachers as far as thousands of miles away from their homes in less than ideal conditions. Predictably, lacking the necessary parental care and support, many of those boys become so malnourished, misled, and abused that they end up as potential recruits for Islamist terror groups and other criminal gangs. To rectify this, the Jonathan administration began the Almajiri School Project—a massive program of construction of schools and hostels, coupled with guaranteed feeding for the Almajiri and salary payments for their teachers.

Anyone would think that such a well-intentioned and relevant project would be a shoo-in. But ten years down the road, not one of those schools is operational and the whole project has been abandoned! Why did this well-intentioned, well-resourced and relevant change iniative fail so spectacularly? The answer lies in the word spelled, c-u-l-t-u-r-e. President Jonathan—a Christian from southern Nigeria—was an "outsider" in Muslim northern Nigeria where the change was being implemented. His outsider's perspective—like the person entering a room with a slight pong—helped him see what needed to be changed, but left him blind to the cultural nuances of Nigeria's Islamic northern region and short of the know-how needed to pull everything off. He thus saw the Almajiri issue as a purely developmental matter requiring only good intentions, relevancy and the channeling of huge sums of money into building projects. But his ignorance of the cultural nuances of Nigeria's Islamic north gendered covert resistance from key stakeholders; resistance which later snowballed into sabotage (one state governor openly refused to commission the Almajiri school in his state!). Again, Professor Schein puts everything in perspective and helps us make sense of the situation, saying,

> The new outside leader must become familiar enough with the old culture to understand just what needs to be changed and what kind of resistance will be encountered. The hybrids as outsiders are in a much better position to figure this out.
>
> The new outside leader *must become familiar enough with the... culture to understand just what needs to be changed and what kind of resistance will be encountered...*

Those words say it all: not understanding the cultural issues at stake was a key reason President Jonathan—a consummate "new outside leader"—failed. Which brings us to the question: if outsiders are unable, and insiders unwilling, to initiate and champion change in a group, what kind of leader is best positioned to do so? The writer of Proverbs proffers an answer, saying,

> I went by the field of the lazy man, And by the vineyard of the man who lacks judgment; And there it was, all overgrown with thorns; Its surface was covered with nettles; Its stone wall was broken down. When I saw it, I considered it well; I looked on it and received instruction: A little sleep, a little slumber, A little folding of the hands to rest; So shall your poverty come like a prowler... (Prov 24:30-34)

These words mean that....

Insiders Often Can't See Why Things Are Going Awry in a System

> *I went past the field of... the man who lacks judgment...*

The vineyard was broken down and the field unproductive, yet the owner (a consummate insider) didn't seem to know *why* things were going awry with his business. This shows that, many a time, a key reason for our lack of judgment—our inability to 'make sense' of the situation— might be the "blindness" that results from our position as insiders. Insiders are like the longtime occupants of a room who can't seem to perceive that the room has an unpleasant odor.

The Successful Implementation of Change Often Requires a Hybrid Leader

> *I* [Solomon] *went past the field of the lazy man...* I considered it well; I looked on it and received instruction [found out why it was broken down]...

To bring change to a broken-down system, Solomon had to first get an idea of what caused the breakdown. And to get an idea of what caused the breakdown, he had to,

> ... [Go] *past* the field of the lazy man.

Notice carefully that Solomon didn't need to go *inside* the field of the lazy man to make his findings. His insight arose from the unique position that being at the border or periphery—not quite inside, and not quite outside—offered. His unusual insight arose from his being a hybrid—someone who's both part-insider and part-outsider. Being part-insider meant that he was acquainted with the nature of the vineyard and accepted by the owner of the business (an outsider would have been seen as untrustworthy and therefore deemed unacceptable to the owner). But being part-outsider also has its benefits because it allows you look at things with an outsider's perspective. Because the hybrid is seen as "one of us" by the insiders, he is acceptable to them. But because the hybrid is also an outsider, he brings the fresh thinking associated with someone from outside the system. These words of the writer of Proverbs show that it's the *hybrid* that's best placed to do the job of pushing the change that challenges a group's deeply held beliefs. Again, Edgar Schein puts all this beautifully, saying,

> The key issue for culture change leaders is that they must become sufficiently marginal in their own culture to recognize what may be its strengths worth preserving and its maladaptive assumptions requiring change...

Changing the Almajiri culture in northern Nigeria, nay, implementing most kinds of major change requires a hybrid leader. The latter is uniquely positioned to recognize the strengths worthy of preservation in the system and the maladaptive assumptions requiring change.

Nevertheless, the words of the writer of Proverbs also offer some hope if you're an insider attempting to bring change to your group. How do I mean? Because,

Crises Often Make People More Open to Change From All Types of Leaders

> *I went past the field of the lazy man...*

Why did the owner of the vineyard allow someone to slowly walk past the walls of his vineyard again and again? Why did he let that person,

> ... consider it well, and look on it?

It was because the vineyard was broken down and in deep crisis

> (....Its surface was covered with nettles; its stone wall was broken down...).

Normally, few persons would grant permission to outsiders to meddle in their business. But the crisis forced the owner of the vineyard to open his business premises to a hybrid (Solomon, the writer of Proverbs) in hope that the latter might find a solution to the problems bedeviling it. In the language of social scientists, we would say that the crisis forced a paradigm shift and made the business owner more willing to accept advice from even total strangers. Harvard's John Kotter puts it brilliantly, saying,

> Visible crises can be enormously helpful in catching people's attention and pushing up urgency levels. Conducting business as usual is very difficult if the building seems to be on fire.

So one way to know whether the change you want to implement is likely to succeed in the face of unfavorable cultural issues, is to simply check to see whether the organization is in crisis (more on the links between change and crises in the next section).

STICKY CHANGE: HOW TO KNOW THAT CHANGE HAS BEEN EMBEDDED IN THE CULTURE

Make Change Stick (Culture Matters)

- Sticky change is change that's not easily reversed or abolished
- Change is sticky when the new practices and behaviors demanded are widely accepted by all members of the group
- Change is very sticky when the new practices and behaviors required are accepted by the most powerful members of the group
- Change is not yet sticky if the new practices and behaviors aren't widely accepted, or are not accepted by powerful group members.

A culture is most powerful when widely shared and deeply held.

—CLAYTON CHRISTENSEN.

Implementing change is tough, so it can be heartbreaking to hear that an initiative you helped birth has come unstuck or been reversed after you left office. This was the case for AlliedSignal CEO Larry Bossidy. In his co-authored book, *Execution: The Discipline of Getting Things Done*, he narrates his experience, saying,

> AlliedSignal had no productivity culture... Our new team conducted the processes with rigor and intensity. By the time I retired... we had tripled our operating margins to almost 15 percent... Putting an execution environment in place is hard, but losing it is easy. Less than two years later, the picture had changed. The company didn't deliver the results... expected...

These words show that, for change not to be reversed or not to undergo wholesale revision or even abolition by another generation of leaders, it must be made *sticky* or be embedded in the culture of the organization. Which brings us to the questions: How do you measure the power, strength or *stickiness* of culture? What does it mean to say that an organization, nation or group has a strong culture? And, most importantly, how do you know that the change you've successfully implemented has been embedded in the culture and will not be easily reversed? As I read psychologist Angela Duckworth's excellent book, *Grit: The Power of Passion and Perseverance*, I began to see some answers from the following words...

> At its core, a culture is defined by the shared norms and values of a group of people. In other words, a distinct culture exists anytime a group of people are in consensus about how we do things around here and why...

PART 3 : THE PRACTICE OF CHANGE

The words that struck me the most are,

> At its core. . . a distinct culture exists anytime a group of people *are in consensus.* . .

In simple terms, a distinct or strong culture develops wherever everyone—leader and follower (without exception)—is equally constrained by the same set of norms or values. This means that weak cultures are those in which some members of the group (usually the powerful and well connected) are exempt from some or all of the norms that constrain behavior. This line of thinking immediately called to mind the famous contest on Mount Carmel between Prophet Elijah and the prophets of Baal. The writer of First Kings provides a lucid account of that incident. . .

> So Ahab sent word throughout all Israel and assembled the prophets on Mount Carmel. Elijah went before the people and said, "How long will you waver between two opinions? If the Lord is God, follow him; but if Baal is God, follow him." But the people said nothing. . . When all the people saw this, they fell prostrate and cried, "The Lord—he is God! The Lord—he is God!" Then Elijah commanded them, "Seize the prophets of Baal. Don't let anyone get away!" They seized them, and Elijah had them brought down to the Kishon Valley and slaughtered there. (1 Kgs 18:20-40)

Much reflection on these words has helped me see the following truths . . .

There Was a Consensus in Israel—a Culture—that permitted the Execution of the Losers of the Kind of Contest that took place on Mount Carmel!

This now-famous contest on Mount Carmel was called by Elijah, acceded to by King Ahab, and accepted by all the people of the northern kingdom of Israel as the way to determine, once and for all, who was really the one true God in Israel. It involved a test where Elijah the representative of Jehovah would call down fire from heaven, and the representatives (prophets) of the contending deity (Baal), would also attempt to do the same. The winner was the person whose principal actually caused fire to fall from the sky and burn up a prepared sacrifice on an altar. As most people know, Elijah (Jehovah's representative) emerged victorious. But what many may not know is that the contest also revealed the prevailing culture in Israel at the time.

Make Change Stick (Culture Matters)

How do I mean? The culture of a group is often revealed by what is widely accepted, allowed and encouraged—or conversely, by what is disallowed or regarded as taboo. By saying,

> ... Seize the prophets of Baal. Don't let anyone get away!" So they [the people] seized them, and Elijah had them brought down to the Kishon valley and slaughtered there,

the writer of First Kings helps us see that there was a consensus among the people of Israel that the losers of this kind of contest were going to pay with their lives! If this wasn't so, the people of Israel wouldn't have obeyed Elijah's instruction to seize the vanquished prophets of Baal and prepare them for execution. More importantly, if there was no such consensus or culture, King Ahab—with all the powers of state at his disposal—wouldn't have stood by and watched as a whopping four hundred and fifty of his own prophets were executed! Therefore we can say that...

Change Has Become Sticky When It Produces a Culture that Can Also Bind and Constrain the Most Powerful Persons in the Group

> So Ahab sent word throughout all Israel and assembled the prophets...

Notice carefully that King Ahab, by sending for the prophets of Baal who were scattered throughout Israel, officially sanctioned the contest on Mount Carmel. Yet even he couldn't save his own prophets from suffering the widely accepted consequence of defeat—death by execution at the hands of a victorious Elijah. Once Ahab had called the contest, even he was bound by the rules of the game. Why? Because culture's power lies in its being widely shared and accepted. In a nutshell, the strength of culture is revealed when even the senior leaders—ostensibly the most powerful members of the group— cannot escape its consequences. It bears repeating: you know that a culture is strong when even the senior leaders of the organization or group aren't exempt from culture's consequences. Therefore, a key way to know that the change you've implemented will last long (be sticky) is to simply check whether it's consequences are binding on, or accepted by, the most powerful members of the group. "*Equal opportunity change*"—change whose consequences are also binding on the most powerful—is change that's sticky. And the reason is not hard to fathom: the most powerful and well-connected are the ones most likely to turn back the hands of the clock!

PART 3 : THE PRACTICE OF CHANGE

Sticky Change Takes Time

The culture was so strong that even King Ahab (the most powerful person in Israel) couldn't escape its consequences—watching helplessly as hundreds of his own prophets were slain. But, and this is crucial, strong cultures are like the proverbial city of Rome—they are never built in a day. Edgar Schein puts it aptly, saying,

> Any social unit that has some kind of shared history will have evolved a culture, with the strength of that culture dependent on the length of its existence, the stability of the group's membership, and the emotional intensity of the actual historical experiences they have shared.

The key phrases in those wise words are:

> ...the strength of that culture [is] dependent on the length of [the group's] existence...

The longer the group's existence, the greater the chances that its culture will become more widely shared and binding on all members—even the most powerful and influential. In essence, embedding change in the culture requires long and tedious hours of work, of communicating, of carefully designing a slew of experiences that must be shared, and of winning people over again and again.

HOW TO MAKE CHANGE STICKY

- Sticky change is change that's intimately linked to the group's reward system
- When it comes to making change stick, the only thing more important than "reward power" is how leaders reward themselves.

> The way leaders reward themselves—as distinct from how they reward others who aren't leaders (and have no power)—is the most potent shaper of group culture.

Probably the most powerful tool leaders can use to shape the behaviors of associates and constituents is their power to reward and punish. If, in the realm of politics and government, the state is defined as the actor with a monopoly of violence in a geographical domain; then we can also say that leaders are, by definition, those persons with a monopoly of 'reward power' in a group. Just like a state subtly uses her monopoly of violence to shape the behavior of citizens, so also do the leaders of a group shape the behaviors of group members by wielding their power to reward and punish. The Psalmist highlighted this age-old truth when he wrote that,

> The wicked freely strut when what is vile is honored [valued; rewarded] among men. (Ps 12:8)

Sticky Change is Change that's Intimately Linked to Reward Systems

> *The wicked freely strut about [without fear of punishment] when what is vile is honored [valued; rewarded] among men.*

The main reason the wicked can freely strut about without fear is that they know they'll never be punished or reprimanded. But, here's the rub: by definition, leaders are persons with reward or punishment power in any group, therefore if the wicked freely strut about, it must be because leaders are unwilling or unable to punish or hold them accountable. This means that leaders can, by using their power of reward and punishment, shape and influence the behaviors of teammates, and bring change to their groups. In simple terms, reward systems are probably the most powerful shapers of peoples' behaviors, and the change that tends to stick is the change that's intimately linked to the reward systems operating in that group. Kerry Patterson and co., in their book, *Influencer: The New Science of Leading Change*, make this clear, saying,

> If bad behavior is *deeply entrenched*, odds are that the current economic system people live in is positively encouraging what you don't want.(Emphasis mine)

The key words in that sentence are,

> ... deeply entrenched... current economic system...

Those words show that the primary way to deeply entrench, embed or make change sticky is via the group's reward system. *Change is made sticky (hard to undo or reverse) when the desired new actions and behaviors are directly linked to the rewards that people can get.*

Although, as we've seen, general reward systems (which reward all) are great for embedding change, there's a specific portion of the reward system that's even stronger at embedding change. It's the reward system *for leaders*. What I mean is this: when it comes to shaping people's behaviors and embedding change, even more important than who is getting promoted or rewarded is this question: how much of the group's resources do leaders—who have the power to reward others—allocate to themselves? The writer of Zephaniah, speaking on this weighty matter, says thus,

> Woe to the city of oppressors, rebellious and defiled! She obeys no one, she accepts no correction. She does not trust in the Lord, she does not draw near to her God. Her officials within her are roaring lions; her rulers are evening wolves, who leave nothing for the morning. Her prophets are unprincipled; they are treacherous people. Her priests... do violence to the law. (Zeph 3:1-4)

From this intriguing quad of verses, we marvel as we see...

A Culture of Rebellion Taking Shape!

> *Woe to the city of oppressors, rebellious and defiled! She obeys no one, she accepts no correction...*

If culture is the way we do things around here, then by,

> ... [obeying] no one,

and

> .. [accepting] no correction,

a culture of lawlessness and disobedience had evolved. Israel had become a terrible place to live, raise kids and do business. As everyone knows, rebellion is a deeply entrenched behavior that's hard to change. The question is: how did this deeply entrenched behavior take root and develop? The answer, as usual, lies hidden in the words of the writer of Zephaniah...

> Woe to the city... *Her officials within her are roaring lions, Her rulers are evening wolves, who leave nothing for the morning...*

These damning words can only mean one thing...

Make Change Stick (Culture Matters)

The Most Deeply Entrenched Behaviors in a Group Are Often the Result of How Leaders Reward Themselves

> *... her officials within her are roaring lions; her rulers are evening wolves, who leave nothing for the morning...*

There it is in black and white: leaders who take the lion-share of resources for themselves

> (... Her officials are roaring lions...),

leaving little for everyone else; and leaders who like,

> ... evening wolves... leave nothing for tomorrow,

build organizations of rebellious and hard-to-correct followers. When leaders take the lion-share of the commonwealth and can't be bothered to put aside something for tomorrow, they not only de-legitimize their leadership in the eyes of followers, they encourage followers and associates to display similar antisocial behaviors. In simple terms, a much ignored way leaders can deeply entrench change is to skew the rewards and benefits that accrue from the change they're initiating in such a way that the lion-share of it goes to followers. Come to think of it, most change initiatives majorly benefit those in authority—a key reason the troops in the trenches don't want them.

When it comes to shaping culture—the way people behave in a group—nothing is more powerful than rewards. I mean, if you want to see a visible change in people's behaviors, simply link the behaviors you desire to visible rewards. If you want sales to improve, simply link salaries and commissions to sales revenue. It is because of this 'reward power'—the control over who gets rewarded or punished—that leaders have such outsized influence in shaping culture. But here's what many leaders don't understand; the only thing greater than 'reward power' in shaping group culture is how leaders reward themselves. *The way leaders reward themselves—as distinct from how they reward others who aren't leaders (and have no power)—is the most potent shaper of group culture.* Why? Because leaders are stewards of organizational resources and how they reward themselves is a window into how they use or abuse power to benefit themselves. If they corner the lion-share of resources, they send out the message that that's the right thing to do—creating a culture of selfish and antisocial behavior throughout the whole group and making it difficult for change to become sticky.

PART 3 : THE PRACTICE OF CHANGE

Wrap Around

Change always requires people to alter or modify their actions and behaviors, but change that requires people to alter deeply held and widely shared beliefs and practices is change that's up against culture. That kind of change genders resistance and opposition and is unlikely to be successful unless leaders take drastic action to push it through. Even then, change that succeeds in spite of cultural opposition is unlikely to 'stick' or become long lasting—being liable to rollbacks, modifications or abolition at the first opportunity. Making change stick requires leaders to link the desired actions to the reward systems operating in their groups. Sticky change is one whose consequences are widely accepted by every member of the group. When the new behaviors demanded by change aren't binding on, or accepted by, the most powerful group members, then that change won't last long.

13

Use Deadlines and Outliers to Raise the Urgency Level

- The best leaders know that urgency is the firelighter for change
- Effective change agents use deadlines to increase the sense of urgency among teammates.
- Outliers are "prophets" and harbingers of change.
- The voices of outliers, when heeded, can help increase urgency in a group.

Urgency discounts the future and values today more than tomorrow; now more than later. It's the key to turning a vision of change into actionable things that must be tackled today.

URGENCY! THE WORD HAS gotten such a bad rap in time management and leadership circles that it's almost considered a four letter word! But, and this is crucial, it's impossible to successfully implement change without a deep and sustained sense of urgency pervading the group. Investment professional Phillip Fisher, in his book, *Common Stocks and Uncommon Profits*, said that,

> What are you doing that your competitors aren't doing yet?" What a great question! *The emphasis was on the word yet...* Most folks, when you ask them that question, aren't doing one darned thing of any great significance their competitors aren't already doing and

Part 3 : The Practice of Change

feel awestruck that you asked them this and they hadn't thought of it themselves. *The firm that is always asking itself that question never becomes complacent. It is never caught behind.* (Emphases mine)

> ...The emphasis is on the word *yet*... The firm that is always asking itself that question never becomes *complacent*...

These words help us see that urgency and complacency are direct opposites. More importantly, they help us see that urgency always shows up in what we're doing now—how we utilize our time today. If it's urgent, then it's pressing and must be attended to today, not tomorrow. *Urgency discounts the future and values today more than tomorrow; now more than later. It's the key to turning a vision of change into actionable things that must be tackled today.*

No change can take root or succeed without the people involved first having a deep and sustained sense of urgency. In his illuminating book, *Upstream: How to Solve Problems Before They Happen,* Duke research fellow Dan Heath narrates the story of entrepreneur and founder of the industrial carpet firm, Interface, Ray Anderson. The latter read a book that assailed the environmentally destructive practices of business leaders and, wait for it, wept! As if weeping wasn't dramatic enough, Mr. Anderson went on to say that,

> I read it [the book which assailed the environmentally destructive practices of corporate leaders], and it changed my life," he said in his memoir. "It hit me right between the eyes.... I wasn't halfway through it before I had the vision I was looking for, not only for that speech but for my company, and *a powerful sense of urgency to do something.* (Emphasis mine)

A galvanized Ray Anderson went on to implement a change initiative that was so far reaching,

> ...one division of Interface... slashed carbon monoxide emissions—from two tons a week to a few hundred pounds per year.

But it all started with,

> ...*a powerful sense of urgency to do something.*

The successful implementation of change always requires a,

> ...*a powerful sense of urgency to do something.*

Use Deadlines and Outliers to Raise the Urgency Level

So how can change agents create a sense of urgency and build a head of pressure to help drive change in the teams they lead? The answer to that question is what we now turn our attention to...

USE DEADLINES TO CREATE, DEEPEN, AND SUSTAIN A SENSE OF URGENCY

A deadline supplies artificial urgency to a task. Consider the April 15 tax deadline in the US. It's an arbitrary date, but it has real power over behavior. About 21.5 million Americans file their taxes in the last week before the deadline. As the deadline looms, you eventually drop everything else and get it done.

—DAN HEATH

Imagine that you're crossing a road and you see a car at a distance—about a mile away—coming slowly at you. You'd be forgiven if, as you leisurely cross the street, you continue eating the chocolate bar in your hand. But, imagine again that, as you lift up your head from the chocolate bar, you suddenly notice that the same car is now just a few meters away—hurtling at very high speed towards you. Suddenly, your attention is focused on the developing situation, and both your stroll and the chocolate bar are pushed to the recesses of your mind as you begin to run for your life. The truth is this: nothing grabs a person's attention like that which is urgent. That which is urgent concentrates the mind, crowds out everything else, and by enabling people to focus on one major theme, makes change easier.

Since an organization or group is made up of many individuals who must work effectively together, and since one of the primal functions of leadership is to direct the attention of subordinates and associates, making things urgent may just be one way leaders can direct the attention and effort of others. Author Robert Greene, in his excellent book, *Mastery*, puts it aptly, saying,

> The feeling that we have endless time to complete our work has an insidious and debilitating effect on our minds. Our attention and thoughts become diffused. Our lack of intensity makes it hard for the brain to jolt into a higher gear. The connections do not occur. For this purpose you must always try to work with deadlines, whether real or manufactured.

In essence, one way leaders can overcome inertia and complacency in the groups they lead is to liberally use deadlines. As I studied the book of Hebrews, I came to better understand how Jehovah—the Leader of leaders—uses the tool of deadlines to, instill a sense of urgency, direct the attention of, and combat complacency, in his church. Listen to the writer of Hebrews. . .

> Not giving up meeting together, as some are in the habit of doing, but encouraging one another—and all the more as you see the Day approaching. (Heb 10:25)

Reflection on this intriguing passage has helped me see the following truths. . .

Deadlines Grab Our Attention Because they Transform What's Important into What's Urgent

> . . . but encouraging one another—*and all the more as you see the Day approaching.*

Did you notice the reason Christians should meet

> ..*all the more* [with greater urgency]*?"*

It's because a deadline is looming:

> . . . *as you see the Day approaching."*

Meetings are *important* in the Christian faith, but they also become *urgent* as the Day (the Second Coming of Christ) gets nearer and nearer. The ultimate deadline, the cut-off mark, the endpoint for all Christians is the Day of Jesus' Second Coming. The closer we get to that deadline, the more it should fill our minds, influence our actions and adjust our priorities. In simple terms, as we see the deadline—the Day of Judgment—approaching, believers should, with greater intensity and urgency, concentrate their efforts on meeting together and encouraging one another. The "deadline" represented by Jesus' Second Coming not only helps us focus on the really important things, it also makes that same important thing—our meeting together—even more urgent. The moral of this passage is this: *people tend to give more attention to tasks with deadlines, to tasks whose deadlines for completion are looming.* Why? Easy. Because the task that was formerly

Use Deadlines and Outliers to Raise the Urgency Level

important now becomes important *and* urgent. And that which is urgent always concentrates the mind and crowds out everything else.

Deadlines drive change, not only because they *clarify what's really important, but also because they "force" us to concentrate our energies and attention on what's most important.* Deadlines make what's important to 'suddenly' become urgent; and it's this *combination of urgency and importance* that's key to getting things done. Urgency drives us to act now, while importance drives us to act *only on the things that matter most,* but deadlines help us act with b*oth urgency and importance.* It's this classic fusion of urgency and importance that gives deadlines the power to both create a sense of urgency and help us focus on the really important things. Following this line of thinking means that, not only must leaders learn to work with time and resource constraints; they must also learn to artificially create the necessary resource constraints that can "force" associates to begin the work of change immediately. You can instill a sense of urgency in the people you lead by gently insisting that they tell you when a job will be completed. For example, the open ended, "I will get back to you," is something to be discouraged. Encourage people to do work that has inbuilt times for accomplishing milestones. Better to accomplish a little every day than to attempt the heart-attack-inducing effort of running a thousand miles on the final day. Begin meetings by stating their aims and durations. If meetings begin to drag, you can make them "standing" meetings—where all participants are on their feet to discourage time wasting. Creating a culture that actively encourages deadlines and milestones is critical to embedding the sense of urgency that can drive change forward in a group. However you act, always keep in mind the following facts,

- Urgency: causes people to act now.
- Importance: causes people to act only on the things that matter but,
- Deadlines: force people to act with both urgency and importance—the very reason deadlines are critical to getting things done.

CULTIVATE OUTLIERS

Outlier: a person or thing situated away or detached from the main body or system.

Part 3 : The Practice of Change

Remember the story of Ray Anderson? He's the entrepreneur and founder of the carpet manufacturing firm, Interface, of whom we spoke about in the first part of this chapter. Recall that he was galvanized to change his company's environmentally destructive manufacturing processes after reading a book. That book was written by a man named Paul Hawken, of whom author Dan Heath said,

> Hawken was an entrepreneur himself—the cofounder of the retail garden chain Smith & Hawken—and he insisted that business leaders had an obligation to reverse course and steer the global economy away from the brink of man-made environmental collapse.

Imagine! An entrepreneur—a person who makes money from doing business; a person with a stake in the way things are currently run—railing against the environmental degradation that business was causing! Paul Hawken was an outlier; a person at the fringes—a person most likely to get it first. *Outliers are like prophets—lone voices crying out to us from the wilderness—urging us to prepare for upcoming change.* They are agents who, when cultivated and heeded, can help instill a sense of urgency in an organization. This brings us to the story of one of Israel's greatest outliers...

GETTING IT FIRST: THE STORY OF RAHAB

Change—in the form of a rampaging army of Israel—was literally bearing down on Jericho. But her inhabitants were having none of it. They'd barricaded themselves in their city and prepared an army to resist it. To a man, they were all against 'change', except for a certain woman called Rahab—a commercial sex worker who, going against the grain, seemed to welcome the Israelites. The story of Rahab, as told by the writer of Joshua, shows us that *some people find it easier to spot and accept incoming change than others.* Why was Rahab so open to change and why was she the only resident of Jericho who saw and welcomed change? And, why did the other inhabitants of Jericho resist the "change" that an Israelite army, who had besieged their city, was bringing? The answers to those questions are hidden in the following words of the writer of Joshua...

> Then Joshua... secretly sent two spies... "Go, look over the land," he said, especially Jericho." So they went and entered the house of a prostitute named Rahab and stayed there... Before the spies

Use Deadlines and Outliers to Raise the Urgency Level

lay down for the night, she went up on the roof. . . Rahab said to them, *"I know that the LORD has given this land to you* and *that a great fear of you has fallen on us, so that all who live in this country are melting in fear because of you. . . We have heard how the LORD dried up the water of the Red Sea for you when you came out of Egypt,* and what you did to Sihon and Og, the two kings of the Amorites east of the Jordan, whom you completely destroyed. . . *.for the house she lived in was part of the city wall.* (Josh 2:1-15)

Much reflection on this passage has helped me see that,

Some People find it Easier to Spot and Accept Incoming Change than Others

By saying,

. . . We have heard how the LORD dried up the waters of the Red Sea,

the writer of Joshua helps us see that everyone, or at least almost everyone that mattered, in Jericho had access to the same information that Rahab possessed—Israel was invincible and change was inevitable. But by going on to say that,

. . . I [Rahab] know that the LORD has given this land to you,"

the writer of Joshua helps us see that only Rahab, of all the citizens of Jericho, could see and accept the change that was about to take place. In effect, we see a much ignored truth: *some people find it easier to spot and accept incoming change than others.* The question becomes: why is this so? The answer is. . .

Rahab Was An Outlier, A Person With Little to Gain From the Status Quo

. . . for the house she lived in was part of the city wall.

There it is in black and white: Rahab was an outsider or outlier to the system that ran Jericho. And the proof is in her address—her house was on the city wall away from the respectable persons and places of Jericho! Sid Buzzel, General Editor of Zondervan, in his biographical entry on the character of Rahab (*Zondervan Leadership Bible*), puts it beautifully, saying,

PART 3 : THE PRACTICE OF CHANGE

> [Rahab], a harlot who lived on the edge of [acceptable] society, was one short stop away from rejection.

In effect, Rahab was an outsider or outlier who had little to gain from the way Jericho was currently run, and therefore owed little or no loyalty to the present order of things. Paraphrasing Machiavelli, Rahab was an ideal candidate for "leading a change in the order of things." Rahab's willingness to accept Israelite spies who had come with the stated aim of overthrowing the system of Jericho shows us the real reason why some people find it easier to start new ventures and implement change...

The People Who Least Benefit from a System Are Least Loyal to it, And More Open to Changing it

Change always demands that you take risks, and the less you already have invested in the current system, the more you are willing to change and try new things. This is why the young who have no name, reputation and riches, and who have little to lose, are often in the vanguard of change. Now that we've seen that it is outliers that are most open to change, we can begin to answer the question, "Why are outliers more open to change?" Interestingly, the writer of the book of Joshua also provides some answers, saying,

> Before the spies lay down to sleep, [Rahab] went up on the roof and said to to them," I know that the Lord has given you this land. . . .We have heard how the Lord dried up the Red Sea. . . (Josh 2:8-13)

Outliers See Things Differently

All the facts stated by Rahab were always in the public domain. The leaders of Jericho, indeed any resident of Jericho, must have heard about the mighty works of God on behalf of the children of Israel. The truth is that they couldn't see what Rahab saw because they had a lot invested in Jericho. Rahab could see differently or, more correctly, was *free* to see differently because she had little going for her in Jericho. This is why it was only a small Swedish drug company that could see the opportunity in the proposal to develop a better ulcer medicine (chapter 8: the Case of Smith, Kline and French). Outliers see things differently. Where others see "threat," they see

Use Deadlines and Outliers to Raise the Urgency Level

"opportunity." But the writer of Joshua isn't done yet. He continues his narrative, saying,

> The [spies] said to her, "This oath you have made us swear will not be binding... unless, when we enter the land, *you have tied this scarlet cord in the window through which you let us down...* "Agreed," she replied... So she sent them away.... *And tied the scarlet cord in the window.* (Josh 2:17-21)

Outliers Don't Much Care About What Others Think of Them

> ... And [Rahab] *tied the scarlet cord in her window.*

Not only did Rahab welcome the Israelite spies, she actually agreed to their demand that she and her family would be spared only if she tied a scarlet cord across her window. Imagine hanging such an unusual cord across her window (had it not been unusual, it couldn't have served as a marker!) People—neighbors, family and friends—must have been curious about the significance of the scarlet cord she'd hung on her window. And they must have peppered her with questions! Rahab—who certainly wouldn't have bothered to answer all those questions—must have been an oddball; willing to be different, to be misunderstood, and to live with ridicule. In short, outliers like Rahab are persons with little need for affirmation from others; persons who can live with rejection and social disapproval. But the writer of Joshua still isn't done yet, he goes on to say that,

> Then Joshua son of Nun secretly sent two spies from Shittim. "Go, look over the land," he said, "especially Jericho." *So they went and entered the house of a prostitute named Rahab and stayed there.* (Joshua 2:1)

These intriguing words help us see another reason for Rahab's openness to change...

Rahab Was the Only Resident of Jericho Who Met the Spies from Israel Face to Face!

> ... So the [spies] went and entered into the house of a prostitute named Rahab and stayed there.

Rahab had firsthand contact with the harbingers of change. The other citizens of Jericho had little or no direct contact with those same agents of change. In modern 'business-speak', we'd say that Rahab was a customer-facing staffer; one whose firsthand exposure to the outside granted her unusual insight into the change that was brewing on the horizon. Outliers are often people who deal directly with the source and carriers of change—a thing that colors their perception of it, and the reason they have a more nuanced view of change. In a nutshell, implementing change comes easiest to leaders who can instill a deep and sustained sense of urgency in their team. And one way to do this is to listen to the "prophets," the outliers who first see change on the horizon.

To be a leader who can step up the urgency level by tapping into the work of outliers,

- Be On the Look Out For, And Listen to, the Rahabs in Your Team: listen to, and cultivate, the outliers in your team. Like we've seen from the story of Rahab, outliers are often customer-facing staff, people whose work puts them in direct contact with brewing change. The leaders who are the best change agents are those who give ear to people like Rahab—people whose lived experiences give great credibility to their warnings and thoughts about brewing change.

- Become Like Rahab: The story of Rahab shows that being a member of the establishment, while in and of itself not a bad thing, can hamper a person's openness to change. To stay open to change, always be guided by this thinking: build your net worth, but hold it lightly. Know that the key to security is not just having things but a willingness to keep changing. Be willing to give up the privileges and position you have accumulated if you have to!

Wrap Around

A deep, sustained and widely shared sense of urgency is a primary distinguishing characteristic of successfully implemented change. This kind of urgency always discounts the future and causes people to act today on the vision of change. Deadlines, because they make what's important to "suddenly" become urgent, imbue people with a sense of urgency. Another overlooked source of urgency are the voices of outliers. The latter are like prophets—people whose position in the social system makes them more

Use Deadlines and Outliers to Raise the Urgency Level

open to sensing and accepting upcoming change. Give ear to them, and you'll probably see the urgency rate go up in your group.

14

Build Credibility and Become a Leader Who Can Make Change Happen.

- When it comes to implementing change, credibility comes before vision. Your credibility with constituents determines whether they'll even accept your vision of change.
- You build credibility by first developing a track record; by walking your talk, by getting some wins under your belt, and by identifying with followers and constituents.

May you have a brilliant idea, which you know is right,
and be unable to convince others.

—OLD ROMANIAN CURSE

CHANGE WILL MOST LIKELY come to pass, not simply because it's done *for* the right people, but majorly because it's done *with* the right people. In other words, no vision for change can become reality except it's able to attract the support of the right caliber of persons. In the old legend of "The Boy Who Cried Wolf," we see a shepherd boy keeping sheep in the field who, because he craved attention or simply wanted to indulge in a prank, cry, "Wolf! Wolf!" The villagers, on hearing his cries, came running to his rescue with their cudgels and knives. Sadly, the villagers found out that it was all a hoax, and there was no wolf. Undaunted, the shepherd boy, still craving attention and not knowing the implications of his actions, decided

Build Credibility and Become a Leader Who Can Make Change Happen.

to pull another fast one, crying, "Wolf! Wolf!" a second time. Predictably, the villagers who came to his rescue found out that there was no wolf in sight. Unfortunately, when a wolf did come to attack the sheep, the shepherd boy's cries of, "Wolf! Wolf!" went unheeded. Why? Because he had lost credibility with the villagers. This story shows the importance of credibility. Leaders who lack credibility find it difficult to get buy-ins from followers and receive little or no support for their projects. In essence, people tend to believe in the leader before they believe in the leader's dream. Leadership expert John Maxwell, in his book, *The 17 Indispensable Laws of Teamwork*, drives home this point, saying,

> . . . Many people who approach the area of vision in leadership have it all backward. They believe that if the cause is good enough, people will automatically buy into it and follow. But that's not how leadership really works. People don't at first follow worthy causes. They follow worthy leaders who promote worthwhile causes. People buy into the leader first, then the leader's vision.

The writer of First Chronicles, in his narrative of David's leadership when God sent an angel to destroy Jerusalem, corroborates this line of thinking, saying,

> And God sent an angel to destroy Jerusalem. But just as the angel was preparing to destroy it, the LORD relented and said to the death angel, "Stop! That is enough!" At that moment the angel of the LORD was standing by the threshing floor of Araunah the Jebusite. *David looked up and saw the angel of the LORD standing between heaven and earth with his sword drawn, stretched out over Jerusalem. So David and the leaders of Israel put on sackcloth to show their distress and fell down with their faces to the ground.* (1 Chron 21:15-16, NLT)

People have to Accept the Leader Before they Accept the Leader's Vision of Change

Did you notice that although it was David *alone* who saw the vision of the angel

> (. . . David looked up and *saw* the angel. . .),

yet all his leaders later put on sackcloth and fell facedown with him in fear and worship (... So David and the leaders... fell facedown)?

The implication is that, after seeing the vision, David must have told his leaders, *who believed him enough to act on what he alone saw!* David had credibility with his leaders—a thing which made them willing to work with him and lend him a helping hand. More importantly, this passage reveals a much overlooked truth: leaders (like David) first find or 'see' the vision and then people who believe in the vision. On the other hand, followers (like David's leaders) first find the leader then the vision. *While many leaders are heard, only a few are believed. Credibility is being both heard and believed.* In mathematical terms, we can state the equation as follows; Credibility= Being Heard + Being Believed.

Credibility Helps Followers Buy into Your Vision

After all is said and done, the reason David's leaders were willing to commit to, and act on, David's vision was simply because they *first* believed in him. Leadership expert John Maxwell puts it beautifully, saying,

> Every message that people receive is filtered through the messenger who delivers it. If you consider the messenger credible, then you believe the message has value." So when leaders ask me, "I have so and so vision, do you think my people will buy into it?" My answer is always, "Do your people buy into you? Do they believe in you?

The answer to the last question, as we see from the experience of David and his leaders, determines whether your people will be committed to your dream of change, and whether the change you are implementing will become reality.

The question on the mind of any discerning reader at this moment must be, "If credibility is so crucial to implementing change, how then can I develop credibility with my people?" The story of Moses offers a perfect answer to that question, and it's to that story that we now turn our attention...

WITHOUT CREDIBILITY: THE STORY OF MOSES

Moses was a leader of Israel who, in a vain attempt to deliver his people from the oppression of the Egyptians, murdered an Egyptian state official. Fearing retribution from the powerful Egyptian king, Moses fled into the

Build Credibility and Become a Leader Who Can Make Change Happen.

vast ungoverned regions of the Midian desert (a little like a modern day Osama Bin Laden fleeing from the face of the American president into the ungoverned deserts of central Asia after the 9/11 attacks). Forty years passed before Moses received a call from the God of the Hebrews to return to Egypt and deliver the people of Israel from the oppression of the king of Egypt. During that long period of time, Moses had lost all contact and credibility with his people. The writer of Exodus helps us see that Moses knew that the main obstacle he faced as he began his leadership journey—his attempt to change the material conditions of the people of Israel in Egypt—was credibility...

> But Moses protested again, *"Look, they won't believe me! They won't do what I tell them. They'll just say, 'The LORD never appeared to you.'"* Then the LORD asked him, "What do you have there in your hand? A shepherd's staff," Moses replied. "Throw it down on the ground," the LORD told him. So Moses threw it down, and it became a snake! Moses was terrified, so he turned and ran away. Then the LORD told him, "Take hold of its tail." So Moses reached out and grabbed it, and it became a shepherd's staff again. *"Perform this sign, and they will believe you,"* the LORD told him. "Then they will realize that the LORD, the God of their ancestors—the God of Abraham, the God of Isaac, and the God of Jacob—really has appeared to you. (Exod 4:1-5, NLT)

Credibility Comes Easiest to Leaders Who Have A Track Record of Success

> *... they won't believe me! They won't do what I tell them...*

There it is in black and white: credibility gets people to believe you and to do what you tell them. It gets people to follow and support you. Notice carefully that God didn't deny that Moses needed credibility to turn his vision for change into reality, instead he wisely instructed him on how to build credibility with a target audience, saying,

> *... Perform this sign, and they will believe you...*

Credibility comes easiest to the leaders who have a track record of success. Or, put in another way, followers are more likely to believe change agents who have a history of getting things done. John Maxwell drives the point home, saying,

> Good leaders always make things happen. They get results... This ability gives them confidence, credibility and increased influence.

Credibility, like all other kinds of influence, takes time and wisdom to build. Get a few wins under your belt and then watch your credibility soar (more on "Generating Small Wins," in chapter 10) Crucially, getting people to buy into your vision doesn't mean that you reach out to everyone simultaneously. It simply means that you *first* reach out to the key influencers. The writer of Exodus makes this clear, saying:

> *Now go and call together all the leaders of Israel. Tell them, 'The LORD, the God of your ancestors—the God of Abraham, Isaac, and Jacob—appeared to me in a burning bush. He said, "You can be sure that I am watching over you and have seen what is happening to you in Egypt." The leaders of the people of Israel will accept your message. Then all of you must go straight to the king of Egypt* and tell him, 'The LORD, the God of the Hebrews, has met with us. Let us go on a three-day journey into the wilderness to offer sacrifices to the LORD our God.' (Exod 3:13-16, NLT)

Credibility With the Masses Begins With Getting Buy-in From Just A Few Key Influencers

> *Now go and call together all the leaders of Israel. Tell them...*

Winning over a large body of persons always begins with winning over the key influencers in the group—the very reason God wanted Moses to *first* gain some credibility with the elders of Israel. Those key influencers would in turn leverage their own influence with the masses and help Moses gain credibility with the latter. Psychologist Adam Grant, in his book, *Originals: How Non-Conformists Move the World,* makes the same point, saying,

> You gain believability by other believable people saying you're believable.

This truth makes implementing change easier because, in the beginning, it helps you focus your efforts on just a few key persons and in this way increases your likelihood of success with the larger group.

Build Credibility and Become a Leader Who Can Make Change Happen.

Wrap Around

Most people think that change begins with a vision; they believe that change starts when they catch or develop a vision. But, because people tend to believe and support a vision only after first believing in the leader behind the vision, one can say that *change begins with credibility. In this sense, we can say that, where there's no credibility, there can be no widely accepted change.* Leaders who lack credibility will struggle to implement change no matter the beauty of the visions they espouse. Credibility comes easily when leaders have a track record of results and a history of identifying with the people they want to influence.

PART 4

Pitfalls and Progeny of Change

OPENING THE BLACK BOX

Black box: in science, computing, and engineering, a black box is a device, system or object which can be viewed in terms of its inputs and outputs... without any knowledge of its internal workings. Its implementation is opaque (black).

—WIKIPEDIA

WHY DO HUMANS OF every race or religious creed have this almost visceral fear of change? Why is the proverbial bird in hand always worth two in the bush? Certainly, it can't be because the bird in hand is the mathematical equivalent of two birds in the bush! Our aversion to change is principally because of all the unexpected events that can pop out when the black box of change is opened—as we begin to implement change. By the way, a black box, in engineering and computer science, is a system whose internal workings are opaque—one in which the only thing over which you have some degree of control is the input mechanism. Because the internal workings are opaque, the system often produces unexpected outputs or results.

It bears repeating: implementing change is akin to opening a black box because of the plethora of unexpected events—positive and negative—that can pop out. Because of our natural aversion to loss—of position, power and prominence—the ushering in of the 'new' and the consignment of the 'old' to history and disuse (the chief effect of change: see chapter 3

Part 4: Pitfalls and Progeny of Change

for the Grandfather Law) is what gives us the most jitters. But change has other unwanted progeny; chief among which are unexpected events like crises, loss of critical assets, failure, disaster, accidents-waiting-to-happen, near misses, uncertainty, random events etc. Sure, we all hope that change will lead to something good or better, but, after all is said and done, it's the prospect of one of these unpleasant and unwanted unexpected events popping out of the black box that makes change seem so scary.

As if the unexpected events themselves aren't difficult enough to handle, leaders also must cope with their unpredictable timing. While most of them *accompany* change, a couple occur *after* change has happened, with some even taking place *before* change starts! All this makes it mandatory for leaders to engage in the difficult work of staying eternally vigilant. But the good news is this: unexpected events can be managed and contained, and the key first step in their management is to understand them. In this section, we begin by looking at crises, and then we take a deep dive into disasters (the mere mention of that word makes me uneasy). We see how Job prepared for a disaster and still lost everything when it finally came. We also learn about near misses (those events that make you exclaim, "Phew! That was close!") from the example of the Israelite tribe of Ephraim. Not done yet, we take another look at the children of Edom who unwittingly laid the groundwork for an accident waiting to happen. We also look at uncertainty and the loss of critical assets—the things most responsible for our visceral fear of change. If Part 1 of this book dealt with the *preamble* or introduction to change, Part 2 with the *principles* of change, and Part 3 the *practice* of change, then Part 4 can be said to deal with the *pitfalls* and *progeny* of change. Why? Because unexpected events can be regarded as the unwanted and unloved children of change.

15

Crisis: the Siamese Twin of Change

MOST PEOPLE INSTINCTIVELY ASSOCIATE change with crises because, not only do they know the old saw about necessity being the mother of invention, but also because many of the changes they've had to make in their personal lives have come only after a crisis. In their minds, crises precede change. The words of Harvard professor John Kotter, in his book, *Leading Change*, epitomize this kind of thinking:

> Visible crises can be enormously helpful in catching people's attention and pushing up urgency levels. Conducting business as usual is very difficult if the building seems to be on fire. But in an increasingly fast-moving world, waiting for a fire to break out is a dubious strategy. And in addition to catching people's attention, a sudden fire can cause a lot of damage... major change is often said to be impossible until an organization's problems become severe enough to generate significant losses.

... major change is often said to be impossible until an organization's problem becomes severe enough...

These words seem to confirm what most people think: a crisis can *cause* or lead to change. But that view is incomplete because the causative arrow can also point backward—*change itself can also cause or lead to crises*. Which is why I often say that change and crisis are like Siamese twins: where you find one, there you'll often find the other. Which brings us to the questions: how exactly does a crisis provoke change? And, how can change provoke a crisis? The following portions of this chapter help us answer both of these questions.

HOW CRISES CAUSE CHANGE

- A crisis is an unexpected event that's also a turning point.
- A crisis can make people more open to seeing things in an entirely new way.

A crisis is a terrible thing to waste.
It can make unthinkable change seem suddenly possible.

—Paul Romer

In the introduction to Part 1, I wrote about Myles Munroe's classification of change into four broad categories. To recap, here's what Dr. Munroe said,

> We generally experience four types of change in life: (1) change that happens around us, (2) change that happens to us, (3) change that happens within us, and (4) change that we make happen.

Dr. Munroe goes ahead to expatiate on each of these categories, saying,

1. Change that happens to us—unexpected or anticipated change that affects our personal lives, families, careers, and so forth.
2. Change that happens around us—unexpected or anticipated change that affects our society, nation, or world and that also has some impact on us personally or on our ways of life.
3. Change that happens within us—unexpected or anticipated change that directly affects who we are—either physically, emotionally, mentally, or spiritually.
4. Change that we initiate—something created or altered by plans we have implemented in order to move us from the present to a preferred future. We can identify each of the above as a distinct type of change, even though, sometimes, there may be overlap between them.

In my opinion, the most powerful kind of change is Type 3—change that happens within us. This kind of *internal* change alters our perspective or the way we see a matter, and empowers us to attempt to change our material circumstances or, in some way, influence the change that happens around, and to, us. In short, internal change (Type 3 Change) is what gives us power over the other types of change. In this sense, *it's internal change (change that happens inside of us) that drives or helps us shape external change (a change in our material circumstances)*. "And how exactly," you may ask, "does this kind of internal change come about?" The Psalmist answers that question saying,

> From the end of the earth will I cry to You, when my heart is overwhelmed and fainting; lead me to the rock that is higher than I [yes, a rock that is too high for me]. (Ps 61:2, AMP)

These intriguing words mean that,

A Crisis Can Produce Internal Change—a Change in Perspective—a Change *in* the Leader

No matter who you are or your station in life, one thing is certain: you'll face challenges, problems and crises. By using the phrase,

> ... *When my heart is overwhelmed and fainting,*

the Psalmist paints the all too common picture of a person emotionally and psychologically overwhelmed by the crisis she's facing. But, by going on to say that,

> ... When my heart is overwhelmed and fainting, *lead me to the rock that is higher than I [yes, a rock that's too high for me],*

he reveals a key benefit of crises: a crisis can change your perspective. An event that leaves you *in extremis* can deeply alter your views about an issue. Look at it like this: climbing to a rock or place higher than where you are right now is symbolic of taking a bird's eye view of the same problem. As almost everyone knows, the way we see the problem (our perspective) from the ground floor is completely different from the way we come to see it when we ascend to the tenth floor of the same building. A bird's eye view from the tenth floor is often very different from the worm's eye view from the ground floor. So what can make us willing to undertake the difficult work of climbing to a higher perch? You guessed right: people are more willing to climb to a rock higher than [them],

or change their perspectives when their

...hearts are overwhelmed,

when they're in a crisis. *A crisis can present people with the ultimate teachable moment and make them more open to seeing things in an entirely new way.* Author Ryan Holliday has this to say about all this,

> What is [perspective]? It's how we see and understand what occurs around us—and what we decide those events will mean. Our perceptions can be a source of strength or of great weakness.

Crises help alter the meaning or interpretation we ascribe to an event and force us to undertake external change. Indeed, even the mere thought of an impending crisis can also produce an internal change in most people! That the crisis (or impending crisis) birthed the change is one reason I often say that change and crises are like Siamese twins—where you see one; there you're most likely to find the other.

A DESPERATE KING SEEKS COUNSEL FROM THE UNLIKELIEST OF SOURCES

Pharaoh King of Egypt had a disturbing dream which none of his counselors could interpret. Deeply troubled, he listened as one of his courtiers told him about an enterprising young man of Hebrew origin who had helped interpret the courtier's dream when both of them were interned in, of all places, the king's dungeon. Desperate for answers, the king sent for the young Hebrew man. The writer of Genesis gives an account of the incident, saying,

> So Pharaoh sent for Joseph, and he was quickly brought from the dungeon. When he had shaved and changed his clothes, he came before Pharaoh. Pharaoh said to Joseph, "I had a dream, and no one can interpret it. But I have heard it said of you that when you hear a dream you can interpret it. (Gen 41:14-15)

The long and short of this story is that, not only was Joseph (the young Hebrew man in question) able to tell Pharaoh the meaning of his dream, he also gave him a plan of action to save Egypt from the impending famine that the king's dream predicted. The king was so pleased that he promoted

Crisis: the Siamese Twin of Change

Joseph and made him governor of Egypt (a position second only to his own)! Again, the writer of Genesis tells the story, saying,

> The plan [proposed by Joseph] seemed good to Pharaoh and to all his officials. So Pharaoh asked them, "Can we find anyone like this man, one in whom is the spirit of God?" Then Pharaoh said to Joseph, "Since God has made all this known to you, there is no one so discerning and wise as you. You shall be in charge of my palace, and all my people are to submit to your orders. Only with respect to the throne will I be greater than you." So Pharaoh said to Joseph, "I hereby put you in charge of the whole land of Egypt." (Gen 41:37-41)

The question in all this is: what made the king and the entire court of an outwardly successful and insular culture like Egypt willing to open up and appoint a total outsider like Joseph to the powerful position of governor? The answer lies in the word, "crisis." The impending crisis of famine and economic hardship predicted by the king's dream made the whole government of Egypt more amenable to the idea of accepting counsel from a rank outsider. The looming crisis changed their perspectives. *It was this internal change in perspective that enabled them make the external change of appointing a total stranger to high office.* Crises represent the classic "teachable moments"—points in time when people are more open to questioning the assumptions and beliefs that power current behaviors. Truly,

> A crisis is a terrible thing to waste, because it makes unthinkable change seem suddenly possible.

Therefore, we can say that, when it comes to change, crises can be of great value because they help produce the internal change that's often the precursor of external change. While a crisis may begin its work "personally"—causing each individual to do a rethink of her actions and helping each person question received wisdom—its work is often completed "organizationally," when groups become more open and amenable to the new and the unfamiliar. This isn't surprising because, after all is said and done, organizational behavior is simply the behavior of the individuals within the group. Having seen how crises (even impending crises) can provoke change, we now turn our attention to the other side of the coin: how change itself can birth crises.

Part 4 : Pitfalls and Progeny of Change

HOW CHANGE CAN BIRTH CRISES

Most people instinctively know that a crisis can lead to change. Indeed, it's this kind of thinking that has given rise to the use of "burning platforms"—using a big crisis to both catch the attention of key stakeholders and generate the urgency needed to implement key change. But many people are oblivious to the fact that the causative arrow can also point backwards—change itself can precipitate crises. The writer of Micah makes this much ignored truth clear, saying,

> But why are you now screaming in terror? Have you no king to lead you? He is dead! Have you no wise people to counsel you? All are gone! Pain has gripped you like it does a woman in labor. Writhe and groan in terrible pain, you people of Jerusalem, for you must leave this city to live in the open fields. You will soon be sent into exile in distant Babylon. . . . (Mic 4:9-10, NLT)

These words are so crucial to gaining a biblical understanding of change that I always insist that people also read them in the Message Translation,

> So why the doomsday hysterics? You still have a king, don't you? But *maybe he's not doing his job and you're panicked like a woman in labor.* Well, go ahead—twist and scream, Daughter Jerusalem. *You are like a woman in childbirth. You'll soon be out of the city, on your way and camping in the open country. And then you'll arrive in Babylon.* What you lost in Jerusalem will be found in Babylon. GOD will give you *new* life again. He'll redeem you from your enemies. (Mic 4:9-10, MSG)

Poorly Led Change Can Birth A Crisis

> . . . You still have a king don't you? *But maybe he's not doing his job and you're panicked like a woman in labor. . .*

Imagine that you're a woman who has been pregnant for the last nine months. Now the time has come for you to deliver your baby. In the middle of the delivery process in the labor ward of your local hospital, you suddenly realize that one half of the attending physicians and midwives are drunk, and the other half are incompetent. You are so vulnerable and panic grips you! Your life and the life of your unborn child are at risk. A normally routine process has become life threatening—has become a huge crisis. All because the midwives of the process can't get the job done.

Using this symbolism of pregnancy, the writer of Micah helps us see that poor management by midwives is one reason the routine change that pregnancy can bring becomes life threatening. By going on to say that,

> You still have a king don't you? *But maybe he's not doing his job,"*

the writer of Micah drives the point home: the change process is like a pregnancy, and leaders are the midwives of change! In other words, improperly managed change can transmogrify into a full blown crisis. In this sense, and drawing from our *pregnancy model* (see chapter 1) a crisis can result from poorly managed change. Change always upends things, but mismanaged or under-led change tends to allow things spiral out of control until they become full blown crises. Which brings us to our next question: how exactly can leaders stop situations from spiraling out of control and becoming full blown crises?

WHY ARE CRISES SO DIFFICULT TO FORESEE OR MANAGE?

- Effective crisis management requires leaders to put up 'strong' responses to 'weak' signals.
- Mismanagement of crises occurs when there's a "crisis-resource mismatch," whenever inadequate resources are "thrown" at an ostensibly "small" problem.
- Managing a crisis requires the creation of a crisis-ready organization—one with a flexible culture that defers to expertise and not rank.
- Leaders in crisis-ready organizations aren't fooled by simplistic diagnoses.

> Complex problems often begin life disguised as simple ones.

Boko Haram!! With tens of thousands dead and millions more displaced, the insurgency in northern Nigeria by the Islamist Boko Haram has gained worldwide notoriety and caused many commentators to ask the question: how come such a serious problem wasn't detected much earlier and nipped in the bud by the Nigerian government? Stepping away from matters Boko

Part 4 : Pitfalls and Progeny of Change

Haram for a moment, that question is also the defining question in crisis management and containment. In essence, why is it so difficult (except in hindsight) to detect or anticipate most crises? Management researchers Karl Weick and Kathleen Sutcliffe, in their excellent book, *Managing the Unexpected*, offer an answer, saying,

> Small events have large consequences... [They]... give off small clues that are hard to spot but easy to treat if... spotted. When clues become much more visible, they are... much harder to treat. Managing the unexpected often means that people have to make strong responses to weak signals, something that is counterintuitive... Normally, we make weak responses to weak signals and strong responses to strong signals.

The phrase that grabbed my attention is,

> ... *Managing the unexpected... means that people have to make strong responses to weak signals...*

In effect, Professors Weick and Sutcliffe are saying that effective crisis management begins when leaders do the counterintuitive thing—respond vigorously to seemingly "harmless" phenomena. The words of the writer of Second Timothy corroborate this line of thinking,

> But shun profane and idle babblings, for they will increase to more ungodliness. And their message will spread like cancer... (2 Tim 2:16-17, NKJV)

These words show that...

Effective Crisis Management Begins When Leaders Put up a Strong Response to Weak Signals

> But *shun profane...* babblings [because]... their message *will spread like cancer...*

Although cancer is a serious and life threatening illness, it often begins as a small, easy-to-ignore and seemingly harmless ailment. Melanomas are one of the most aggressive and dangerous forms of cancer, but, and this is crucial, they often begin as small, easy-to-ignore black spots on the skin.

By using the metaphor of cancer to describe the threat posed by,

> ... profane and idle babblings,

Crisis: the Siamese Twin of Change

the writer of Second Timothy highlights the essential nature of crises: they can spread rapidly, but often begin as small easy-to-ignore incidents. But by going on to say that,

> *shun* profane ... babblings,"

He advocates that leaders put up a vigorous response at the *initial* stage of a crisis. The word, "shun" means to persistently avoid and to give a wide berth to something— pretty strong words on how to handle a "small matter" like idle talk! But when that "small matter" can, *like a cancer*, spread and engulf everything in sight, one understands why a strong initial response is necessary.

Effective Crisis Management Requires that Leaders Avoid Simplistic Diagnoses

> ... their message will spread *like cancer*...

Cancer often first presents as a simple fever, a small painless lump or a small sore—misleading even the most skillful diagnosticians into thinking it's only a simple disease they're confronting. I remember the case of one well known attorney here in Nigeria who, for a long time, was believed to be a person living with chronic pneumonia (a disease of the lungs). It wasn't until much later that his doctors found out that what they mistook for pneumonia was actually lung cancer! The small, barely visible crack in a wall may well be the outward sign of bigger problems with the foundation of the building. Leaders who effectively manage crisis aren't fooled by simple explanations: they know that *complex problems often begin life disguised as simple ones*—the very reason they put up 'strong' responses to 'weak' signals.

Effective Crisis Management Requires that Leaders Defer to Expertise

> ... their message will spread like cancer...

Just like the treatment of cancer always requires the engagement of qualified medical specialists, so the management of crisis also requires expertise. Indeed, it's interesting to note that operatives of Nigeria's secret service

(DSS) were the first to spot the threat posed by Boko Haram—warning their political masters in a series of expert reports many years ago. It's impossible to contain a crisis without requisite knowledge, and groups that don't possess resident experts must hire outsiders.

Effective Crisis Management Occurs Best In Organizations With Flexible Cultures

The containment of crisis—like the containment of cancer—always requires expertise, and because these experts are often not in positions of authority within the organization, their counsel is often ignored and discounted. Professors Weick and Sutcliffe put it beautifully, saying,

> Expertise is not necessarily matched with hierarchical position, so organizations that live or die by their hierarchy are seldom in a position to know all they can about a problem.

The implication is that leaders need to be flexible—willing to put aside hierarchy and embrace expertise! They need to search all levels of the organization to find out who has the requisite expertise to handle the current crisis. Psychologist James Reason, in his excellent book, *Managing the Risks of Organizational Accidents*, underscores this point, saying,

> A flexible culture takes a number of forms, but in many cases it involves shifting from the conventional hierarchical mode to a flatter professional structure, where control passes to task experts on the spot, and then reverts back to the traditional bureaucratic mode once the emergency has passed. Such adaptability is an essential feature of the crisis-prepared organization...

Simply put, organizations that can become flatter in the face of crisis are more likely to triumph.

Crisis Mismanagement Occurs Whenever There's A Crisis-Resource Mismatch

In the beginning, a crisis—like a cancer—is hard to detect and easy to resolve but, and this is crucial, in the end, it always becomes easy to detect and hard to resolve! Why? Because a crisis often begins by giving off weak signals—seducing leaders into responding weakly by using only a small amount of resources to deal with a supposedly "small" problem. In the early stages, leaders often have the resources to nip the crisis in the bud, but their weak response allows the crisis incubate and gather strength until it snowballs into chaos—at which time the resources required to handle the matter may be unavailable. In every case, it is this "crisis-resource mismatch"—not throwing enough resources of men, materiel and money at the problem—that allows things to spiral out of control. This crisis-resource mismatch is writ large in the management of the Boko Haram insurgency: a billion dollars spent today seems like a drop in the bucket, but could have made all the difference ten years ago!

Egypt was one of the ancient world's great powers, and it's not surprising that her leaders were probably the best in that era. It's to one of those leaders that we now turn to better understand the phenomenon of "crisis-resource mismatch."

THE CASE OF PHARAOH KING OF EGYPT AND AN IMPENDING FAMINE

Recall the story of Pharaoh, the king of Egypt whose dream was interpreted by Joseph. The former's dream predicted seven years of plenty that was to be followed by another seven years of famine. The famine was going to be so severe that it would seem as if it had not been preceded by seven years of plenty. In effect, the famine was going to leave Egypt (the so called Granary of the Ancient World) economically devastated. Listen as Joseph informs Pharaoh of his plan of action to tackle the famine,

> And now let Pharaoh look for a discerning and wise man and put him in charge of the land of Egypt. Let Pharaoh appoint commissioners over the land to take a fifth of the harvest of Egypt during the seven years of abundance... to be used during the seven years of famine that will come upon Egypt, so that the country may not be ruined by the famine... 'You [Joseph] shall be in charge of my palace, and all my people are to submit to your orders. Only with respect to the throne will I be greater than you.' (Gen 41:33-40)

Pharaoh Skillfully Manages A Crisis

Now, keep in mind that this was really only a dream—the ultimate 'weak signal' for most people—yet Pharaoh responded vigorously and really shook up things! He appointed Joseph to prepare for the famine by storing up grains from the seven years of plenty. Not only did the king respond vigorously, but by also telling Joseph, "*... Only with respect to the throne will I be greater than you,*" the king effectively was deferring to Joseph's expertise! Managing a crisis, whether in an ancient kingdom or in a modern organization, requires leaders who defer to expertise, lead groups with flexible organizational cultures, and do the counterintuitive—put up a strong response to weak signals. Pharaoh exemplifies that kind of leadership. Thank God for leaders like him.

Wrap Around

A crisis can, in the words of change expert John Kotter, be regarded as a "burning platform"—something that grabs attention and causes people to rethink their former actions and values. The chief benefit of a crisis is its ability to cause internal change in people, to change the meanings they ascribe to the events occurring around them and then push them to engage in external change. To further complicate matters, crises don't only cause change, they're also caused by change. As if that isn't enough, crises hardly ever show up fully formed—they often begin life as small easy-to-ignore signs that demand vigorous responses. It's a failure to put up the required vigorous response that allows things spiral out of control and become the "burning platforms" with which we are all so well acquainted.

16

Disaster vs Crisis

What Disasters Really Are

- A crisis is an unexpected event that's also a turning point.
- A disaster is more than just a crisis, it's a misfortune that requires more resources than is currently available to you before it can be mitigated or resolved.

I explained the difference between disaster, where there is no choice left, and crisis, a critical turning point...

—MAX MCKEOWN

ALTHOUGH MANY PEOPLE ARE aware that crises belong to the category of what social scientists refer to as unexpected events, they often confuse crises with disasters. UCLA professor and bestselling author Jared Diamond, in his book, *Upheaval: Turning Points for Nations in Crisis*, offers probably the most illuminating definition of crises when he said,

> How do we define a "crisis"? A convenient starting point is the derivation of the English word "crisis" from the Greek noun "krisis" and verb "krino," which have several related meanings: "to separate," "to decide," "to draw a distinction," and "turning point." Hence one can think of a crisis as a moment of truth: a turning point, when conditions before and after that "moment" are "much

PART 4 : PITFALLS AND PROGENY OF CHANGE

more" different from one another than before and after "most" other moments.

> *... One can think of a crisis as a moment of truth: a turning point, when conditions before and after that "moment" are much more different from one another than before and after "most" other moments.*

Those words say it all: a crisis is a turning point or opportunity that can birth change. So what's a disaster, and how is a disaster different from a crisis? The writer of Micah throws some light on that question, saying,

> Therefore, the LORD says: "I am planning *disaster* against this people, *from which you cannot save yourselves*. You will no longer walk proudly, for it will be *a time of calamity*. (Mic 2:3)

Disasters Are Different—In Degree And In Kind—From Crises

By saying,

> I am planning *disaster* against this people, *from which you cannot save yourselves*,

the writer of Micah helps us see that a disaster is an unexpected event of such magnitude that our resources alone can't solve, mitigate or navigate. In this sense, a disaster is different both in kind and in degree from a crisis. Disasters, being misfortunes are different in *kind*; and being periods of intense emotional and financial pressure that cannot be surmounted by our own resources, are different in *degree*. Again, a crisis is both opportunity and danger, but a disaster is essentially only a misfortune or calamity. The writer of Proverbs drives the point home, saying,

> Do not forsake your friend and the friend of your father, and do not go to your brother's house *when disaster strikes you*—better a neighbor nearby than a brother far away. (Prov 27:10)

His words show that,

Disaster vs Crisis

Disasters Are Contrary Circumstances that Your Resources Alone Can't Handle Or Resolve

> ... and do not go to your relative's house when *disaster* strikes you— better a neighbor nearby than a relative far away.

Implicit in these words is this truth: *when disaster strikes, a person always needs external help!* Go to,

> ... a relative far away,

or go to,

> ... a neighbor nearby...

Whatever the case, a disaster forces a person to seek external help because the resources in his own house, organization or network aren't enough to cope with the problem. Disasters gulp plenty of resources. But, here's the rub, one person's disaster is another's minor problem. How can this be? Easy. The difference lies in the varying volumes of resources available to each of us! It bears repeating: *a disaster is more than just a crisis, it's a misfortune that requires more resources than is available to you before it can be mitigated or resolved* (if not so, the writer of Proverbs wouldn't have advised us to get help from close neighbors). Disasters are a peculiar type of unexpected event that do plenty of damage and demand plenty of resources—more resources than you possess—the reason they often force you to fall back on your social network. Disasters leave people or groups enfeebled.

Disasters Leave You With Little Or No Wiggle Room

> ... and do not go to your brother's house when disaster strikes you— better a neighbor nearby than a brother far away.

Disasters leave us with little wiggle room. A person facing a disaster or calamity has no choice but to go out and look for help. Strategy teacher Max McKeown, in his excellent book, *Adaptability: The Art of Winning in an Age of Uncertainty,* drives this point home, saying,

> I explained the difference between disaster, where there is no choice left, and crisis, a critical turning point...

Part 4 : Pitfalls and Progeny of Change

Disasters Expose the Nature and Strength Of Our Social Networks

> *Your own friend and your father's friend* do not forsake. In the day of disaster, better a *neighbor* that is near than a *brother* far away.

The terms, "Your own friend and your father's friend," "neighbor," and "brother," say it all. Surviving a disaster requires you to fall back on the people within your social network. This means that disasters are brutal tests of the quality and strength of a person's relationships and social networks. Psychologist Charles Perrow, in his book, *The Next Catastrophe*, stresses this point, saying,

> Disasters expose our social structure and culture more sharply than other important events. They reveal starkly the failure of organizations, regulations, and the political system. But we regard disasters as exceptional events, and after a disaster we shore up our defenses and try to improve our responses while leaving the target in place. (Emphasis mine)

If this is true, then it means that...

Disasters Are Emergencies that Force Leaders to Fall Back on the Relationships they've Built Prior to that Time

> ... do not go to your brother's house when disaster strikes you— better a neighbor *nearby* than a brother *faraway*.

> ... *nearby*. ... *faraway*...

Those contrasting words help us see that disasters can happen so quickly that little or no time is available to make the journey to ask help from a brother who is far away! Disasters are emergencies that require leaders to leverage the relationships they've already built with their neighbors. In this sense, disaster management begins long before the disaster takes place. It begins when leaders cultivate the relationships of neighbors by investing in them. All this leads us to the life of a man named Job, a man who suffered the hellish loss of all he had in a disaster. But Job wasn't naive; he had a premonition of what was coming to him! How do I know this? Because Job displayed "mindfulness."

MINDFULNESS

If eternal vigilance is the price of liberty,
then chronic unease is the price of safety.

—James Reason

Managing unexpected events always begins with what psychologists refer to as 'mindfulness'—a healthy awareness or preoccupation with what can go wrong. Recently on Facebook, I saw a post by a friend explaining how she'd just noticed a small black mole on her leg. That observation, according to her, was evidence of how little we know about ourselves. While many of her Facebook friends oohed and aahed in delight, alarmed, I "in boxed" her and told her to have the spot medically checked because it could be a melanoma (an aggressive cancer that usually begins as a small innocuous black spot on the skin). Because unexpected events, like many cancers, often begin small before becoming full blown and life- or career-threatening, early detection is the critical first step in their management. The writer of Proverbs drives this point home, saying,

> A prudent person sees trouble coming and ducks; a simpleton walks in blindly and is clobbered. (Prov 22:3, MSG)

These words mean that...

Mindfulness—A Healthy Preoccupation With What Can Go Wrong—Is the First Step to Managing the Unexpected

Managing the unexpected begins with *mindfulness*, with being aware of what can go wrong—which helps spot trouble or danger afar off. By saying,

> A prudent person *sees*... and... a simpleton walks in *blindly*,"

the writer of Proverbs contrasts the behavior of the prudent with that of the simpleton. The former is aware of upcoming danger because his eyes are wide open—looking for the things that can go wrong; while the latter is blind and naive. In essence, prudence, because it is mindful of the things that can go wrong, is better able to detect and manage unexpected events. Researchers Karl Weick and Kathleen Sutcliffe said that,

Mindfulness increases as people become more conscious about the ways in which the system can be disrupted, *what might go wrong*, and who these disruptions are likely to harm. And when mindfulness increases, people are less likely to deny that unexpected surprises can happen or to rationalize away the potential consequences. (Emphasis mine)

Clearly, what Drs. Weick and Sutcliffe refer to as "mindfulness" is what the writer of Proverbs refers to as "prudence." All this calls to mind the leadership of Job. Few persons in the Scripture record suffered from disaster more than Job. I mean, Job literally lost everything—wealth, health, family and friendships; so much so that the book of Job could rightly be called the book of Disaster! As I began to study the management of unexpected events, I was surprised to see that Job was a mindful leader. Listen to the writer of Job. . .

What I always feared has happened to me. What I dreaded has come to be. (Job 3:25, NLT)

These amazing words can only mean that,

Job Exhibited Mindfulness—A Healthy Preoccupation With What Can Go Wrong!

What I always feared has happened to me. . .

There it is in black and white: Job was "mindful"—deeply aware of what could go wrong *long before it went wrong!* He correctly anticipated that he could face certain events that could wipe out his business! But mindfulness is more than just anticipation, more than just,

The prudent.[foreseeing]. . . trouble coming,

it's also taking action to protect yourself from what you think can go wrong. Interestingly, a close study of the words of the writer of Job reveals that Job actually attempted to protect himself from the disaster he envisaged!

One day when Job's sons and daughters were feasting and drinking wine at the oldest brother's house, a messenger came to Job and said, "The oxen were plowing and the donkeys were grazing nearby, and the Sabeans attacked and made off with them. They put the servants to the sword, and I am the only one who has escaped to tell you!" While he was still speaking, another messenger came and said, "The fire of God fell from the heavens and burned up the sheep and the servants, and I am the only one who has escaped to tell you!" While he was still speaking, another messenger came and said, "The Chaldeans formed three raiding parties and swept down on your camels and made off with them. They put the servants to the sword, and I am the only one who has escaped to tell you!" (Job 1:13-17)

These words show that...

Job Attempted to Protect Himself From Disaster By Hedging His Bets—By Spreading His Assets Over Multiple Locations

> One day... a messenger came... While he was still speaking another messenger came... While [the second messenger] was still speaking, [a third] messenger came...

Taken together, these words help us see one thing: *the messengers came in from three different locations.* In other words, Job did not put all his eggs in one basket. By locating oxen and donkeys in grazing areas separate and far from either sheep or camels, Job hedged his bets and spread his risks—making it less likely that all four valuable assets (oxen, donkeys, sheep and camels) would be destroyed in one fell swoop. Indeed, by going on to say that,

> ... The Chaldeans formed *three raiding parties* and swept down on your camels,

the writer of Job shows us the great lengths to which Job went to protect his assets—even dividing his valuable camels into *three separate groups* in order to make it less likely for all of them to be rustled at the same time. In effect, Job was mindful, alert and aware of the threats posed to his business by marauding bands of cattle rustlers (Sabeans and Chaldeans) and took steps to protect himself from those threats. Although, ultimately, he was overwhelmed by scale of the disaster that befell him, the fact remains that from the get-go; Job was mindful and correctly anticipated what could go wrong.

Mindfulness Rides on the Wings of Expertise

The main reason I was able to quickly detect that the tiny black spot on my Facebook friend's skin could be a melanoma was because of my training as a healthcare practitioner. Job could correctly predict the threats to his business because he was skillful in agribusiness. In much the same way, mindfulness works best when you have some knowledge in a particular vocation or when you avail yourself of the knowledge of experts. Mindfulness is definitely not suspicion or superstition.

Job Did Face A Disaster!

Recall that a disaster is more than just a crisis; it's a misfortune that requires more resources than is available to you before it can be mitigated or resolved. If so, the following words of the writer of Job offer conclusive proof that Job faced a disaster...

> When Job prayed for his friends, the LORD restored his fortunes. In fact, the LORD gave him twice as much as before! Then all his brothers, sisters, and former friends came and feasted with him in his home. And they consoled him and comforted him because of all the trials the LORD had brought against him. And each of them brought him a gift of money and a gold ring. (Job 42:10-11)

> ... the Lord restored [Job's] fortunes... Then [at that time] all his brothers, sisters, and former friends came [to] him... *And each of them brought him a gift of money and a gold ring.*

Nothing can be clearer than this passage! Job was only able to recover from the disaster because of the gifts of material resources which he received from family and friends. Disasters gulp resources, and surviving them requires that leaders tap into their social networks.

Wrap Around

Probably the most dangerous class of unexpected events to pop out of the black box of change is disasters. Disasters are different in kind and degree from crises. The latter are turning points that can, in the short-term, produce internal change (a change in our perspectives) and, in the long-term, external change (a change in our circumstances). On the other hand, disasters are calamities that require huge amounts of resources to rectify and

Disaster vs Crisis

resolve—more resources than currently at our disposal. They are best managed by a character quality that psychologists refer to as mindfulness—a vigilance that seeks out what can go wrong long before it occurs—and by developing requisite relationships with key friends and allies long before the disaster strikes.

Job was mindful; correctly foreseeing that cattle rustlers posed the greatest threat to his business. For leaders who prefer to look only on the bright side of things, being mindful is unnatural, unpleasant, counterintuitive and difficult. Being mindful is a preoccupation with failure that involves answering these five questions:

1. What needs to go right?
2. What can go wrong?
3. How can things go wrong?
4. What things have already gone wrong?
5. What actions have I taken to protect myself or my team from the negative effects of questions 1-4?

17

Near Misses, Close Calls, And Accidents Waiting to Happen

NEAR MISSES

- Near misses and close calls are harbingers of disaster.
- A near miss is a sign of vulnerability in a system or process.
- Near misses are signs that you're depending on luck or chance.
- Near misses are failures dressed up as success, wolves in sheep's clothing.
- Near misses require leaders to do more than heave a sigh of relief; they should reflect and alter their behaviors.

Near miss: A successful outcome in which chance or some other factor plays a role in averting disaster.

SOMETIME AGO, AS I bent forward to open the deep freezer to cut myself a slice of beef, I forgot that I was holding the knife with the point turned upwards and almost stabbed myself in the eye! Thoroughly shaken by such a close shave with serious injury, subsequent reflection revealed all my foolish missteps—opening the freezer with an upheld knife in one hand while, at the same time, bending to reach for the meat in the dark; and using an old freezer with no inner lights. Like I said before, implementing change is like opening a black box and near misses—like the one that happened to

Near Misses, Close Calls, And Accidents Waiting to Happen

me—are simply one type of unexpected event that can pop out. My close shave with serious injury as I leaned into the deep freezer, was not only a wakeup call, it also helped call to mind the OSHA (Occupational Safety and Health Administration) definition of a near miss,

> An incident in which no property was damaged and no personal injury was sustained, but where, given a slight shift in time or position, damage or injury easily could have occurred.

Interestingly enough, the words of the writer of Amos agree with that definition,

> I overthrew some of you as I overthrew Sodom and Gomorrah. You were like a burning stick snatched from the fire, yet you have not returned to me," declares the Lord. (Amos 4:11)

These words help us see that...

Near Misses Are Harbingers of Disaster

> I overthrew some of you as I overthrew Sodom and Gomorrah.
> *You were like a burning stick snatched from the fire...*

A burning stick snatched from the fire is the ultimate picture of near destruction. It's a picture of something that was almost totally destroyed, but somehow survived. It's the symbol of the near miss or close shave. By contrasting the case of Sodom and Gomorrah—cities that suffered total destruction—with the case of a near miss

> ... a burning stick snatched from the fire,

the writer of Amos shows us that total destruction is often closely connected with near misses. In simple terms, before every "Sodom and Gomorrah" incident, there probably was a burning-stick-snatched-from-the-fire incident. Before people suffer total destruction, they often experience a near miss. Therefore, one way we can know that there's something amiss with a process or system is the near miss, the close call, the result you get that makes you exclaim, "Phew, that was close!" Near misses are harbingers of disaster simply because they often show up a few times before disaster happens.

PART 4 : PITFALLS AND PROGENY OF CHANGE

Near Misses Require Leaders to Stop, Reflect And Make A U-Turn

By saying,

> ... You were like a burning stick snatched from the fire, *yet you have not returned to me,*

the writer of Amos helps us see that God expected Israel's leaders to "return" to Him—to reflect on, and learn lessons from, what happened, and then make a U-turn after their close shave with trouble. Near misses are wake up calls to stop and reflect on the integrity of your processes. If you're implementing change and you experience a near miss, then you need to take a closer look at the whole process. In essence, change agents who experience near misses ought to do more than heave a sigh of relief; they need to realize that their success is probably due to luck or chance and, more importantly, they also need to scrutinize their actions to see what they're doing wrong. Why? Because next time when luck runs out, there'll likely be a disaster and not a near miss.

A Near Miss is Failure Disguised as Success

Why is it that leaders who experience the high of being like,

> ... a burning stick snatched from the fire,

of being "miraculously" delivered from certain disaster, never deem it necessary to "return" to God, or to reflect and alter their behaviors? It's because they are deluded into seeing their close shave as a validation of their previous actions, rather than objectively assessing the near miss as a failure disguised as success. Seeing an event as a success means that I'm little inclined to modify it. Seeing the same event as failure disguised as success (like my narrow escape from self-inflicted blindness) forces me to review my operations. Near misses are wolves in sheep's clothing!

Learning from a Near Miss is Akin to Taking a Vaccine

A vaccine is an attenuated or weakened version of a microbe which, when injected into the human body, provokes our immune system to produce a slew of biochemicals to protect us from the microbe in question—without killing us. The key phrase in that sentence is, "without killing us." Since near misses don't kill, damage or destroy, learning from them is like taking

Near Misses, Close Calls, And Accidents Waiting to Happen

a vaccine shot. Psychologist James Reason communicates the point beautifully, saying,

> A near-miss is any event that could have had bad consequences, but did not. If the right conclusions are drawn and acted upon, they can work like '*vaccines*' to mobilize the system's defenses against some more serious occurrence in the future—and, like good vaccines, they do this without damaging anyone or anything in the process. (Emphasis mine)

In effect, learning from near misses can 'vaccinate' an organization against some more serious occurrence in the future. With these truths in mind, we now turn our attention to a group of persons in the Scripture record who refused to learn from a near miss—and paid a terrible price!

> Then the men of Ephraim called out their forces, crossed over toward Zaphon, and said to Jephthah, "Why did you cross over to fight against the people of Ammon, and did not call us to go with you? We will burn your house down... Now Jephthah gathered together all the men of Gilead and fought against Ephraim. And the men of Gilead defeated Ephraim... *There fell at that time forty-two thousand Ephraimites.* (Judg 12:1-6)

Disaster! Forty-two Thousand Killed in a Civil War!

Jephthah the Gileadite, Israel's hotheaded leader, was heading home after defeating the Ammonites in battle, when an equally hotheaded group of armed Ephraimites accosted him. The latter demanded to know why, in the first place, Jephthah didn't call them to help fight the Ammonites. In the ensuing argument, tempers flared and, as is usual with heavily armed and hotheaded men, weapons were drawn and a military showdown occurred. After the fog of war had cleared, and with Jephthah victorious, a staggering 42,000 Ephraimites lay dead! To the cursory reader, this shocking bloodletting looks like a one-off disaster. But a close study of the book of Judges reveals a near miss involving this same Ephraimites many years before. Listen again to the writer of Judges,

> Now the men of Ephraim [the same tribe that accosted Jephthah] said to [Gideon], "Why have you done this to us by not calling us when you went to fight with the Midianites?" And they reprimanded him sharply. So he said to them, "What have I done

now in comparison with you... Then their anger toward him subsided... (Judg 8:1-3)

Before the Disaster, There Was a Near Miss!

This passage puts things in perspective: helping us see that the Ephraimites always had it coming to them! Before the disastrous war that led to the loss of 42,000 Ephraimite lives in the twelfth chapter of the book of Judges, there was this close shave, this near miss, when the same Ephraimites almost came to blows with another leader of Israel—Gideon—who also was returning from battle! Their unwillingness or inability to learn from this near miss and deal with their underlying wrong behavior made disaster inevitable. The reason the Ephraimites weren't massacred in this first altercation with Gideon is in hindsight all too clear: it was purely the result of chance—Gideon was restrained and coolheaded. Not learning from the near miss with a coolheaded Gideon made the disaster with Jephthah (an original hothead) inevitable. When we learn to *not* interpret near misses as successes, and see them for what they really are; failures disguised as success and harbingers of catastrophe, we become better at managing unexpected events and navigating change.

CORRECTLY MANAGING NEAR MISSES REQUIRES LEADERS WHO ARE WILLING TO ARGUE WITH RESULTS

When you're confronted with failure, it's natural to ask why disaster struck. Unfortunately success doesn't trigger such soul-searching. Success is commonly interpreted as evidence not only that your existing strategy works, but also that you have all the information and knowledge you need.

—GARY PISANO AND FRANCESCA GINO

I have always taken it for granted that one cannot argue with results, and that results speak for themselves, so imagine my astonishment when, as I read management researchers Catharine Tinsley, Robin Dillon and Peter Madsen's Harvard Business Review article, *How to Avoid a Catastrophe*, I came across these eye-opening words,

Near Misses, Close Calls, And Accidents Waiting to Happen

> When people observe a successful outcome, their natural tendency is to assume that the process that led to it was fundamentally sound, even when it wasn't: hence the common phrase, "You can't argue with success" In fact, you can - and should.

As I reflected on the import of these weighty words, I came to better understand why the common saying "You can't argue with results" is so off the mark from, of all places, the book of Numbers! Listen to the writer of Numbers as he tells the story of a leader who on the surface, appeared to have unquestionable results, but who in reality was only a short step away from career suicide...

> And Moses and Aaron gathered the assembly together before the rock; and he said to them, "Hear now, you rebels! Must we bring water for you out of this rock?" Then Moses lifted his hand and struck the rock twice with his rod; and water came out abundantly, and the congregation and their animals drank. Then the Lord spoke to Moses and Aaron, "Because you did not believe me, to hallow me in the eyes of the children of Israel, therefore you shall not bring this assembly into the land which I have given them. (Numbers 20:10-12, NKJV)

Moses Gets Results!

> ... Then Moses lifted his hand and struck the rock twice with his hand, and water came out abundantly, and the congregation and their animals drank...

Imagine being at the head of a thirsty three-million-person strong organization in a desert. Certainly, your back must be against the proverbial wall. Then imagine taking the staff in your hand and striking a rock twice and seeing water flow abundantly for all to drink! Undoubtedly, that result should speak for itself. But trouble was brewing for Moses as the words of the writer of Numbers later reveal...

PART 4 : PITFALLS AND PROGENY OF CHANGE

You Should Argue With Results When the Process that Produced the Results is Shaky, Dependent on Chance, or Unethical

> . . . *Because you did not believe me, to hallow me in the eyes of the children of Israel, therefore you shall not bring this assembly into the land which I have given them.*

With these grim words, we come to see that not only did God rebuke Moses for his behavior; he also punished him by denying him entry into the Promised Land. Moses was supposed to *speak* to the rock, but he *struck* the rock. Although he obtained results, the real problem was the process through which the results came. This example certainly takes the hammer to the saying, "You can't argue with results." Researchers Gary Pisano and Francesca Gino, in their Harvard Business Review article, *Why Leaders Don't Learn From Success*, said that,

> When you're confronted with failure, it's natural to ask why disaster struck. Unfortunately success doesn't trigger such soul-searching. Success is commonly interpreted as evidence not only that your existing strategy works, but also that you have all the information and knowledge you need.

In simple terms, when most of us see a successful outcome we assume that it must be the fruit of a successful process. But as the example of Moses reveals, leaders can obtain results even when they do wrong! The writer of Romans agrees with the thinking of Pisano and Gino, saying. . .

> For if the truth of God hath more abounded through my lie unto His glory; why yet am I also judged as a sinner? And not rather, (as we be slanderously reported, and as some affirm that we say,), Let us do evil that good may come? Whose damnation is just. (Rom 3:7-8, KJV)

These words mean that. . .

In the Economy of God, Means and Ends Must Always Align to the Highest Ethical Standards

This amazing passage shows us clearly that God is not only concerned with the 'ends' (results), he is also equally concerned with the 'means' (methods) with which we obtain our results. A leader cannot say,

Near Misses, Close Calls, And Accidents Waiting to Happen

> Let us do evil [use unethical means/methods] in order that, or as long as, good results [ethical ends] come about.

Leaders are responsible for ensuring that they use the right means to achieve the right ends. *Even if—like Moses striking the rock—the truth of God has abounded through your "results" to his glory, you are still counted as a sinner!* Management writer Stephen M. R. Covey drives this point home, saying,

> The means are as important as the ends. How you go about achieving results is as important as the results themselves...

The key questions to ask yourself every time you taste success and obtain results are these: Did I follow legal and ethical methods to obtain my results? Is there some element of luck or chance driving the process? Do environmental factors or the incompetence of competitors account for some of the success I experienced? These questions help locate the real reasons for your success and also ensure that your results are reproducible and sustainable—and they help you learn from near misses. Whatever, the best leaders always keep in mind this truth: You can argue with results!

ACCIDENTS WAITING TO HAPPEN

We've all at some point heard someone say, "It was an accident waiting to happen"—meaning that there was something hidden or latent about the situation that increased the likelihood of the occurrence of an accident. Psychologist James Reason has the following to say about accidents waiting to happen,

> Latent conditions are to... organizations what resident pathogens are to the human body. Like pathogens, latent conditions—such as poor design, gaps in supervision... maintenance failures... shortfalls in training, less than adequate tools and equipment—may be present for many years before they combine with local circumstances and active failures to penetrate the system's many layers of defenses.

Professor Reason is saying that just like the Tubercle bacillus can lie dormant in a human for many years before causing life threatening tuberculosis, so certain factors can lie hidden in our lives before precipitating crises. *It is the presence of these latent factors that transforms an otherwise* normal situation into the 'accident waiting to happen'. The writer of Obadiah, in his missive against the Edomites (a nation of people closely related to the Hebrews), agrees with this, saying,

> If thieves came to you, if robbers in the night— oh, *what a disaster awaits you!*— would they not steal. . . as much as they wanted?. . . (Obad 1:5)

An Accident-Waiting-to-Happen Situation Develops

> . . . oh, *what a disaster awaits you!..*

Those words say it all: the Edomites had allowed a situation that was a disaster-waiting-to- happen to develop. They were so exposed that if robbers attacked at night, they would lose everything. To use Professor Reason's metaphor, there was a "hidden pathogen" or latent condition in their set-up that made them vulnerable to attack and destruction. The question becomes: what was the latent condition that made the Edomites so vulnerable? The answer, as usual, lies hidden (pardon the pun) in the words of the writer of Obadiah. . .

> The pride of your heart has deceived you, you who live in the clefts of the rocks and make your home on the heights, *you who say to yourself, 'Who can bring me down to the ground?'* Though you soar like the eagle and make your nest among the stars, from there I will bring you down," declares the Lord. "If thieves came to you, if robbers in the night— oh, what a disaster awaits you! (Obad 1:3-5)

Edom's Pride Birthed an Accident Waiting to Happen

> . . . *you who say to yourself, 'Who can bring me down to the ground?'*

Undoubtedly, Edom's overconfidence—her thinking that because she lived in a high and lofty fortress, no one could ever defeat her in battle—was the latent factor that made her vulnerable. Since pride goes before a fall, it's easy to see why Edom's overconfidence acted as a latent factor. But the writer of Obadiah isn't done yet, he goes ahead to show exactly how latent factors made Edom vulnerable, saying,

Near Misses, Close Calls, And Accidents Waiting to Happen

> *All your allies will force you to the border; your friends will deceive and overpower you; those who eat your bread will set a trap for you, but you will not detect it. (Obad 1:7)*

Latent Factors Set the 'Accident Sequence' in Motion By Forcing Us to Operate Under Borderline Conditions

> *All your allies will force you to the border. . ."*

Latent failures make you vulnerable because they, in the words of Professor Reason,

> *. . . set the accident sequence in motion,*

by forcing you to operate at the borderline. Borderline operations are operations undertaken with little or no reserves; they are operations where there's little or no margin of error and safety to handle emergencies. It's like being chased by a lion *after* you've just completed a marathon, or like running a business that faces a huge financial crisis *after* many years of making losses. Organizations operating at the borderline are so feeble they are unable to handle emergencies and crises. Indeed, by saying that,

> All. . . your *allies* [not even, your enemies] *will force you to the border,"*

the writer of Obadiah drives home the point: very little pressure is needed before things breakdown in a system with latent failure.

Latent Factors Blind Us to Reality

> *. . . those who eat your bread will set a trap for you, but you will not detect it.*

Latent faults disconnect us from reality by blinding us to what's going wrong, even when the wrongdoing is perpetrated by friends with whom we're familiar. In short, wherever there's a latent fault in a system, even the familiar trips us up. Not detecting wrongdoing automatically means that leaders are unable to right them—further worsening an already bad situation. *The crucial damage that latent factors do is not just that they enfeeble the organization, but that also they blind leaders and make them unaware that their organization is weak—until it is too late!*

Latent Failures vs Active Failures

Imagine a workman operating a machine in a factory who drops his spanner into the machine, an action which causes all work to immediately grind to a halt. That kind of failure with its *immediate* consequences is described as an active failure and is often produced by operators or low-level staff. In contrast, latent failures may lie unnoticed for years before precipitating crises. So which group of persons is responsible for latent failures? The writer of Obadiah proffers an answer, saying,

> In that day," declares the Lord, "will I not destroy the wise men of Edom, those of understanding in the mountains of Esau? (Obad 1:8)

These words mean that...

Latent Failures Are the Handiwork of Top Management

> ...*will I not destroy the wise men of Edom*...

Because Edom's leaders were the source of her pride and conceit, they were responsible for the latent conditions that ultimately led to her fall. In essence, latent faults are a byproduct of the actions of top management. If accidents waiting to happen are the result of the actions of top management, what actions must change agents take to reduce their incidence? The occurrence of accidents waiting to happen can be reduced by...

Building 'Slack' into Systems and Processes

> All your allies will force you to the *border*...

Because the 'accident sequence' kicks off whenever people or systems operate under borderline conditions—conditions in which there are no reserves or 'slack' to deal with emergencies—deliberately engineering slack into your operations is one way to derail the accident sequence. For example, setting aside financial reserves can protect you from the vagaries of unexpected events. In other words, systems or processes without slack are accidents waiting to happen!

Stress Testing

Nothing reveals the strengths—and hidden weaknesses—of a system like stress. Under pressure, what's inside and hidden tends to become exposed for all to see. In fact, the latent pathogens that cause disease in humans often need stressors like illness and fatigue before they can do damage. The best leaders sniff out accidents waiting to happen by deliberately subjecting their systems to simulated stressors. They can do this by simply reducing the quantity of a key component that their systems or people need to operate—and then observe the results. This is the origin of the stress tests that financial regulators use to reveal hidden weaknesses in banks and other financial institutions.

Wrap Around

Implementing change always opens a black box. The latter contains a combo of unexpected events. One type of unexpected event that change agents can experience is the near miss. Unlike other unexpected events which bring loss, pain and regret, near misses might even be sources of joy! Why? Because a close shave with failure or a project that succeeds by chance can be interpreted as success. But the truth is that near misses are harbingers of disaster because they often show up just before the latter occurs. Accordingly, experiencing a near miss while implementing change should be a source of concern. Close shaves demand that leaders stop, reflect, and learn. Accidents waiting to happen, on the other hand, are latent or hidden conditions that predispose a system to failure. Their presence is often only revealed in hindsight by failure. Detecting and removing them requires a great deal of introspection and testing (e.g., stress testing to reveal unseen weaknesses in operations).

18

Managing the Loss of Critical Assets

- Failure and loss are the hallmarks of change gone awry
- The management of loss begins with knowing that the loss of critical assets only makes what's left more valuable.
- The ability to find and put the resources you still have left to work is key to managing loss.

And when critical resources have been lost, the most important asset an organization can possess is easy access to the resources it has left.

—Duncan Watts

FAILURE AND THE ACCOMPANYING loss of critical assets are two of the items in the black box of change that give us the most jitters. I mean, who hasn't heard about people who lost all they had simply because of some change that occurred at work or in the marketplace, or even because of some change they initiated that spiraled out of control. So the question is not whether failure and loss of critical assets can accompany change, but how can one manage such failure and loss if and when they occur? To answer the last question, let's carry out the following thought experiment...

Imagine that you are worth exactly two million dollars in cash which you stashed in a safe at home. Imagine again that a fire sweeps through your house—burning everything in its path. On getting home, you are only able to salvage one million dollars of your money—all the remaining notes were burnt to ashes. There is no insurance. Tears well up in your eyes at your loss. The weeping continues until you receive some sage advice from a mentor that helps you see that what's left—the one million dollars untouched by the blaze—is *now* more valuable to you!

Understanding that what's left after a loss is not only more valuable, but is also the key to restoration and recovery, is the critical first step to managing the loss of critical assets. The words of the Preacher of ancient Israel bear this out...

> Two are better than one, because they have a good return for their labor: If either of them falls down, one can help the other up. But pity the man who falls and has no one to help him up. (Eccl 4:9-10)

This intriguing passage helps us see that...

The Management of Loss Begins with Understanding that what's Left After a Loss Is Now More Valuable than Before

> ... *If either of them falls down, one can help the other up.* ..

There it is in black and white: the key to surviving the fall, failure or loss of the first partner is in the second partner (it's the latter that can help the former to his feet). This means that when a critical asset is lost, the assets that remain immediately assume greater importance and become even more valuable. Why? Because they are the assets which, when put to use, can help you recover from your loss. Not appreciating this truth is a principal reason many leaders become discouraged and throw in the towel after a major loss of assets.

The Ability to Quickly Put the Remaining Resources You Have to Work is Key to Managing Loss

> Two are better than one... If either of them falls down, one can help the other up..

Did you notice that reviving the fallen partner required that the partner unaffected by adversity immediately go to work? Surviving the loss of a critical asset is hugely dependent on your ability to immediately, or as soon as possible, begin to put your remaining assets to work. Sociologist and

PART 4 : PITFALLS AND PROGENY OF CHANGE

former Microsoft researcher Duncan Watts, in his book, *Six Degrees: The Science of a Connected Age,* drives the point home, saying,

> And when critical resources have been lost, the most important asset an organization can possess is easy access to the resources it has left.

Although the loss of critical assets can be psychologically damaging, it can be managed by a firm decision to locate the assets that remain after the loss and to begin putting them to work. Imagine my astonishment when I realized that this principle was used by the prophet Elisha as he helped a certain widow recover from financial loss. The writer of Second Kings narrates that story, saying,

> The wife of a man from the company of the prophets cried out to Elisha, "Your servant my husband is dead, and you know that he revered the Lord. But now his creditor is coming to take my two boys as his slaves." Elisha replied to her, "How can I help you? Tell me, *what do you have in your house?*" "Your servant has nothing there at all," she said, "except a small jar of olive oil. (2 Kgs 4:1-2)

Quickly Putting to Work What's Left was Key to a Widow's Recovery from Loss

In this famous passage of Scripture, we see Elisha the prophet help a destitute widow overcome the loss of her husband and breadwinner, and pay off a huge financial debt by, you guessed right, helping her put what was left after the loss—a small jar of oil—to work. By saying,

> Elisha replied to her, "How can I help you? Tell me, *what do you have in your house?*"

the writer of Second Kings helps us see that Elisha knew that what's left after a loss is crucial to managing the loss of critical assets. In contrast the widow's response to Elisha's query,

> Your servant has nothing there at all, except a small jar of olive oil,

shows her ignorance of that principle. The writer of Second Kings continues his narrative, saying,

> Elisha said, "Go around and ask all your neighbors for empty jars. Don't ask for just a few. Then go inside and shut the door behind

Managing the Loss of Critical Assets

you and your sons. Pour oil into all the jars, and as each is filled, put it to one side." She left him and afterward shut the door behind her and her sons. They brought the jars to her and she kept pouring. When all the jars were full, she said to her son, "Bring me another one." But he replied, "There is not a jar left." Then the oil stopped flowing. She went and told the man of God, and he said, "Go, sell the oil and pay your debts. You and your sons can live on what is left." (2 Kgs 4:3-7)

The long and short of the story is this: the widow realizes that, although she'd suffered the loss of a husband and breadwinner, was mired in debt arising from a failed venture, and was now facing a "repo" of her two sons by cold-hearted creditors, she still had something valuable left at home—a jar of precious olive oil. Although, God performed a miracle of supernatural increase when he multiplied the oil as it was being poured out into many borrowed vessels, the truth is that, the widow's financial restoration was kick started by putting to work what remained after she suffered a loss. In essence, the losses the widow suffered made the ". . . small jar of olive oil," even more valuable to her family.

Wrap Around

When it comes to implementing change, failure and loss of critical assets come with the territory. When faced with a loss of critical assets. . .

1. Begin by taking stock of what's left: After suffering a loss, the best leaders take stock of what's left because they know that what's left is key to restoration and,

2. Quickly put what's left to work: Ask yourself, "How can I better utilize what's left?"

Doing #1 can also cause you to be grateful that everything wasn't destroyed!

19

Managing the Uncertainty that Always Accompanies Change

- Implementing change is like opening a black box—full of uncertainty.
- Uncertainty involves random or chance events and is the 'mother' of risk.
- Navigating change requires that change agents understand the concepts of risk, random events or chance occurrences.
- Navigating change requires that you manage uncertainty which, in turn requires you to value and tolerate interruptions.

THE PROCESS OF IMPLEMENTING change is often so fraught with unwanted or unexpected events, that it can be likened to opening the proverbial black box. Indeed, one can say that, when it comes to implementing change, the only thing certain is that change always comes accompanied with uncertainty! And uncertainty, as any businessperson knows, implies risk. Kick-starting a new initiative means that you're likely to experience a plethora of results—ranging from the intended and the unintended (random or chance), to the consequential and inconsequential. It's this increased likelihood of failure or getting an unexpected result that makes change (or even the mere thought of leading change) so enervating for many. Success and experience don't seem to blunt or decrease the shivers that change gives us; on the contrary, they heighten it. When we are just starting out with no name, no money in the bank and few of the trappings of success, we have little to lose and are ready to risk it all. But with a little success and some name recognition, we do have something to lose and we become a little skittish about bearing risk and implementing change. Because, as we've seen in the Grandfather Law, change is the principle of life, we must press on. But pressing on requires that we manage—by first understanding—the uncertainty, risk, randomness and chance events that always accompany change. The writer of Ecclesiastes, a man also known as the Preacher of ancient Israel, using the decidedly agrarian picture of seed sowing, helps us better understand uncertainty, risk, and randomness, saying,

> Sow your seed in the morning, and at evening let your hands not be idle, *for you do not know which will succeed, whether this or that, or whether both will do equally well.* (Eccl 11:6)

Much reflection on these intriguing words has helped me see the following truths...

Uncertainty Lurks Wherever We Cannot Control Outcomes; Whenever Sowing Doesn't Guarantee Reaping

> *Sow your seed... For you do not know which will succeed...*

For all those who think harvest *automatically* follows sowing [Genesis 8:22], these words are unsettling! Ideally, reaping should follow sowing, but by saying,

> ... for you do not know which will succeed,

the Preacher introduces us to a peculiar situation where sowing doesn't guarantee reaping. What does this mean? It means that, if you can't get a guaranteed harvest after sowing your seed, then you must be dealing with uncertainty, chance or randomness. In effect, these words of the writer of Ecclesiastes are a primer on managing uncertainty and risk—the things which always accompany change.

Uncertainty Arises From Incomplete Information

> ... for *you do not know* which will succeed...

These words hit the nail on the head. They help us see what exactly it is that makes an event uncertain, random or a chance occurrence. It's when we

PART 4 : PITFALLS AND PROGENY OF CHANGE

...do not know,

or can't tell whether the event or investment of effort will succeed or fail. In essence, uncertainty operates at the twilight zone of our ignorance. In this light, statistician and investor Nicholas Nassim Taleb was correct when he said that,

> What is random and what you do not know are functionally the same.

The less we know about how something operates, the more the uncertainty we have to deal with and vice versa.

Uncertainty is the Mother of Risk

> *... you do not know which will succeed, whether this or that, or whether both will do equally well.*

Because there's uncertainty, one can't know for sure which of the projects (the seed sown in the morning or the seed sown in the evening) will succeed or fail. In simple terms, the greater the uncertainty, the greater the risk or probability of failure associated with the project, and the more cautious the change agent should be.

Symmetric Risk Occurs Whenever Multiple Independent Events Have Different Probabilities of Success

> *...* for you do not know which will succeed, *whether this or that, or whether both will do equally well.*

When the success or failure of one project is independent of others, and when the occurrence of one event is *not* a game-changer, then you're dealing with symmetric risk.

Symmetric Risk is Associated with Steady Growth and Accumulation

> *...* Sow your seed in the morning, and at evening let your hands not be idle...

Managing the Uncertainty that Always Accompanies Change

In a symmetric risk scenario, no single event has the power to overly impact or influence results. Symmetric risk-taking is like planting a crop—one harvest builds upon another and you certainly don't expect windfall wealth. If you're in a business where your income today is related to your income yesterday and to the effort you put in, then you're engaged in a business that carries symmetric risk. So how do you manage symmetric risk? Listen again to the Preacher...

Managing Symmetric Risks Requires Patience And Persistence

> ... Sow your seed in the *morning,* and at *evening* let your hands not be idle...

To win in a business or profession with symmetric risk, you must stay in the game, you must be patient and persistent—willing to remain at the task from morning to evening. If one endeavor fails, pick yourself up and start another. Here the saying, "Failure is never final" applies (it doesn't necessarily apply with *asymmetric risk* where one failure can wipe you out; which we will look at subsequently). So next time you hear the saying, "Failure is never final," just smile and say to yourself, "It depends on what kind of risk you're taking." Why? Because failure in a game full of asymmetric risk can be final and fatal!

Managing Symmetric Risks Requires 'Modular' Planning—the Placing of Multiple Small Bets

> Sow your seed in the morning, and at evening let your hands not be idle for you do not know which would succeed...

When you don't know which option or action will succeed and when all options have an equal chance of success, then you're better off sowing as many seeds as possible...

> In the morning sow the seed, and in the evening withhold not your hand...

In short, you manage symmetric risk by increasing the number of your bets—which simultaneously increases your probability of success. Each "bet" or project must be modular in nature—small and wholly independent of the others. Psychologist Gary Klein, in his book, *The Power of Intuition*, drives this point home, saying,

> Another way to reduce uncertainty [risk] is to reduce the complexity of the plan you are formulating. For example, you can make your plan more modular so the tasks can stand on their own. (The contrast is to a very interactive plan where one task influences another.) A modular plan lets you gain flexibility. The failure of one part may not endanger the others.

Having seen how symmetric risk operates, we can now turn our attention to asymmetric risk...

MANAGING ASYMMETRIC RISK

... the skewness issue; it does not matter how frequently something succeeds if failure is too costly to bear.

—Nassim Taleb

Nigerian history between 1966 and 1999 was blighted by the deadly game of chance called military coups. The potential upside of a coup—capture of state power—was significantly lower than its downside—death by firing squad. Every time the potential downside of an action significantly outweighs the potential upside, you're dealing with asymmetric risk. In effect, all the 'coupists' of that sordid era were dealing with asymmetric risk. A simple way to understand the logic behind asymmetric risk is to carry out the following thought experiment. Imagine that you're calculating the average net worth of a large sample of Americans. As you input the figures into your computer, it seems as if no single value is capable of greatly affecting the average—until you come to Amazon boss Jeff Bezos! At $196 billion, the latter's net worth tips the scale. Not taking it into account can seriously impair the accuracy of your result.

Statisticians would say that that sample is skewed—just a few measurements are majorly responsible for the final results. Although the measurements which can skew your sample are very rare (there aren't that many Jeff Bezoses), not taking them into account can leave you with a grossly inaccurate final figure. The downside of rare events in asymmetric risk are like the Jeff Bezoses in your sample or the firing squad for failed coupists;

Managing the Uncertainty that Always Accompanies Change

when they do occur, they can wipe out all past gains and upend all previous calculations. Interestingly, the Preacher has something to say about asymmetric risks,

> Dead flies will cause even a bottle of perfume to stink! Yes, an ounce of foolishness can outweigh a pound of wisdom and honor. (Eccl 10:1, NLT)

These cryptic words drive home the point...

Asymmetric Risk Occurs Whenever the Negative Impact of One Event Greatly Outweighs the Positive Impact of Many Other Events

As a pharmacist who took courses in cosmetology, I know that it takes great skill to make a bottle of perfume. But all that wisdom comes to naught if but one dead fly is allowed to enter the bottle. Why? Because the sweet smell of perfume is quickly replaced by a stench. The Preacher compares these "dead flies" to, "*an ounce of foolishness,*" which "*outweigh a pound of wisdom and honor.*" He means to say that the plenty of wise actions needed to make a bottle of perfume can be undone by a small and improbable act of foolishness that lets in a dead fly. The impact of many acts of wisdom being outweighed by just one tiny act of foolishness is evidence that we're dealing with a skewed sample or asymmetric risk. Remember that in a skewed sample, a single measurement (which occurs rarely) outweighs many other measurements (which occur frequently). The former are game-changers whenever they occur, as the writer of Proverbs also lets us see...

> Men do not despise a thief if he steals to satisfy his hunger when he is starving, yet if he is caught, he must pay sevenfold, though it costs him all the wealth of his house. (Prov 6:30-31)

Asymmetric Risk Lurks Wherever All Previous Gains Can Be Wiped Out By A Single Bad Result

Stealing is risky business. Thieves are seldom caught, and the potential upside (reaping where you didn't sow) can make stealing attractive to some. But when a thief is caught, the downside—paying back sevenfold and losing all one's wealth—is far greater than the upside. All the resources which the thief 'accumulated' in a long career is wiped out in one fell swoop. This proverb reveals the essence of asymmetric risk; all the gains you've made can be wiped away with one "bad luck" event! But the writer of Proverbs isn't done yet, using the example of sexual infidelity, he goes ahead to show us how to manage asymmetric risk, saying,

> But a man who commits adultery *lacks judgment*; whoever does so destroys himself. . . . (Prov 6:32-35)

Don't Play the Game If Asymmetric Risk Is Present!

Adultery (sleeping with another man's wife etc.) is a form of stealing which, if you engage in it *often enough*, will be found out—and in which the downside significantly outweighs the upside, The writer of Proverbs categorically declares that a man involved in the asymmetric risk associated with adultery is ". . . [lacking in] judgment," or foolish. This advice is borne out by the experience of the over 500 soldiers who have died or been executed in the aftermath of military coups in Nigeria! I have read a lot about what some respected management scholars refer to as "Big Hairy Audacious Goals," or "betting the company." These are actions that often entail betting everything on one single turn of the wheel or one change initiative. If the downside of that kind of initiative can result in the 'death' of your enterprise, then the risk is asymmetric and the words of the writer of Proverbs argue against such a move.

If you've played a Game with Asymmetric Risk and Won, Then it's Time to Stop!

Although an initial run of success is possible when dealing with asymmetric risk, sooner or later the game-changing rare bad-luck event will happen and wipe away all your previous gains. So if you've ever played in a game with asymmetric risks and won, it's time to take your winnings and run!

If implementing change is akin to opening a black box—full of uncertainty—the question becomes: how can change agents manage the uncertainty that's sure to accompany the change they want to implement? One answer lies in the word, "interruptions," the subject to which we now turn our attention.

Managing the Uncertainty that Always Accompanies Change

THE VALUE OF INTERRUPTIONS

An interruption is anything that prevents the start-to-finish completion of a critical task.

—Tim Ferris

Interruption! The word has almost become a dirty word in leadership and time management. A fact which writer Tim Ferris, in his bestselling book, *The Four Hour Workweek*, drives home when he said that,

> An interruption is anything that prevents the start-to-finish completion of a critical task.

Mr. Ferris's definition is probably the reason most leaders detest interruptions; after all, no one likes anything that can prevent the start-to-finish completion of a critical task! But imagine that you're presiding over a meeting deliberating on the facts being marshaled by a speaker and someone signals that another person has some more *current* information on the matter at hand. What do you do? If you're like me, you'll politely signal to the speaker to give way to the person with the latest information. Management writer Henry Mintzberg, in his thought provoking book, *Managing*, drives this point home, saying,

> Why this preference for interruption? To some extent, managers tolerate interruptions because they do not wish to discourage the flow of *current* information.(Emphasis mine)

Professor Mintzberg's words show us exactly why many practicing leaders love interruptions: it's because they believe that interruptions help them stay abreast of a situation by giving them access to the latest information. Interestingly enough, the words of the writer of Proverbs agree with this line of thinking,

> Every enterprise is built by wise planning, becomes strong through common sense and profits wonderfully *by keeping abreast of the facts."* (Prov 24:1-3, TLB)

Making A Profit Demands that Leaders Always Stay Abreast of the Facts

> *...profits wonderfully by keeping abreast of the facts.*

Did you notice where the profit lies? It lies in staying current or keeping abreast of the facts. The underlying assumption is not only that you need facts to turn a profit, but also that the facts of the business at hand are volatile and subject to change. Clearly then, leaders who don't stay abreast of the facts inevitably suffer punishment and loss. The question becomes, how exactly can leaders keep abreast of rapidly changing facts? The writer of First Corinthians answers that weighty question, saying,

> Two or three prophets should speak, and the others should weigh carefully what is said. *And if a revelation comes to someone who is sitting down, the first speaker should stop.* (1 Cor 14:29-30)

Reflection on these words has helped me see that...

Interruptions Allow New and More Current Information to be Injected into the Decision-making Process

> *...And if a revelation* [new or more current information] *comes to someone who is sitting down, the first speaker should stop.*

There it is in black and white: interruptions to the order of speaking or to the information flows at meetings are allowed whenever leaders realize that helpful, new and task-relevant information from other credible sources are now available. In effect...

Interruptions Give Leaders the 'Manager's Advantage'—Helping them Stay Up to Date

> Two or three prophets [experts] should speak, and the others should weigh carefully what is said. And if a revelation [new information] comes to someone who is sitting down, the first speaker should stop.

Managing the Uncertainty that Always Accompanies Change

These words help us see the value of interruptions—they help leaders stay abreast of the events occurring around them. Again, Professor Mintzberg sums it up, saying,

> ... the manager's advantage lies not in documented information, which can be made available to anyone, but in the *current, not (yet) documented information* transmitted largely by word of mouth—for example, the gossip, hearsay, and opinion discussed... Indeed, much of an informed manager's information is not even verbal so much as visual and visceral—in other words, seen and felt more than heard, representing the art and craft of managing more than its science. Effective managers pick up tone of voice, facial expression, body language, mood, and atmosphere.

Professor Mintzberg's wise words show us why an isolated manager—a manager no one can reach—is invariably an ineffective manager.

The More Fluid And Unstable the Situation, the More Leaders Must Tolerate Interruptions

Certainly, leaders who operate in sectors that face little change should strive to reduce interruptions to the barest minimum. But those in sectors buffeted by rapid change must develop a high degree of tolerance to it. Indeed, *they must see interruptions as a key to managing or navigating change!* If you're leading in a stable or slowly changing environment or are engaged in creative work, then interruptions probably are a pain in the neck because they prevent the start-to-finish completion of critical tasks (see chapter 10 for 'Maker's Schedule' vs. 'Manager's Schedule'). But if you're leading in a more volatile environment, then interruptions must be tolerated—or even cultivated—because they help inject the latest information into your decision-making process. In essence, how leaders see interruptions is determined by the environment in which they operate.

A LEADER FAILS TO STAY ABREAST OF THE FACTS, AND PAYS WITH HIS LIFE (THE STORY OF GENERAL SISERA)

Little causes, they say, can have big effects. But little causes are often the products of slight shifts in circumstances—a slight change in buyer specifications or a slight delay in one's knowledge of the latest facts of the matter. The proverbial fog of war—which blinds soldiers from clearly seeing the rapid, but ever so slight, changes in battlefield conditions—provides probably the best example of how little causes can deeply influence a leader's ability to navigate the turbulence, uncertainty and fluidity that always accompany change. Sisera was commanding General of a Canaanite army; an army that was locked in mortal combat with the army of Israel. Winning the war against Israel, like winning most other wars, required the help of allies. And Sisera could count on his alliance with the Kenites to help him defeat the Israelites. That alliance provided him with intelligence, supplies, and a refuge in time of trouble. The writer of Judges shows just how crucial the alliance was to Sisera, saying,

> There Barak [commander of the army of Israel] summoned Zebulun and Naphtali, and ten thousand men went up under his command... *when they told* Sisera that Barak son of Abinoam had gone up to Mount Tabor, Sisera summoned from Harosheth Haggoyim to the Kishon River all his men and his nine hundred chariots fitted with iron. (Judg 4:10-13)

General Sisera's Access to the Latest Intelligence Keeps Him One Step Ahead of the Enemy

> ... *when they told* Sisera that Barak son of Abinoam had gone up to Mount Tabor..

There it is in black and white: General Sisera's superb intelligence contacts were spot on—informing him about enemy mobilization and troop movements. The general knew that enemy troops under the leadership of the Israelite General Barak were taking positions on the strategic Mount Tabor, so he summoned all his men and his armored chariots to lay ambush for them on the way. Having access to the latest intelligence helped Sisera stay one step ahead of the enemy. But as soon as the battle was joined, the situation began to degenerate and Sisera was now on the back foot—fleeing from the battlefield on foot! Listen again to the writer of Judges, as he continues his narrative,

> Sisera, meanwhile, fled on foot to the tent of Jael, the wife of Heber the Kenite, *because there was an alliance between Jabin king of Hazor and the family of Heber the Kenite...* Jael went out to meet Sisera and said to him, "Come, my lord, come right in. Don't be afraid." So he entered her tent, and she covered him with

Managing the Uncertainty that Always Accompanies Change

> a blanket. . . "Stand in the doorway of the tent," he told her. "If someone comes by and asks you, 'Is anyone in there?' say 'No.'" But Jael, Heber's wife, picked up a tent peg and a hammer and went quietly to him while he lay fast asleep, exhausted. She drove the peg through his temple into the ground, and he died. (Judges 4:17)

General Sisera Meets His End—Not On the Battlefield, But At the Hands of an Ally Turned Enemy!

> . . . She drove the peg through his temple into the ground, and he died.

Those words say it all: Sisera, commanding General of the Army of Jabin king of the Canaanites was killed, not on the battlefield, but in his sleep by a woman in a tent! The question becomes: why did Sisera trust this woman in the first place that he even slept off in her tent? The answer lies buried in the following words of the writer of Judges. . .

> . . . "Sisera, meanwhile, fled on foot to the tent of Jael, the wife of Heber the Kenite; *because there was an alliance between Jabin king of Hazor and the family of Heber the Kenite.* . .

These words show that. . .

General Sisera Ran into Heber's Tent because there was an Alliance between His Country and the Kenites

There was an alliance between Sisera's king and the Kenites, an alliance that should normally have offered Sisera protection from his pursuers. But, the situation was so fluid that Sisera happened to have lost track of a certain small change in the facts on ground before the battle started. Listen to the writer of Judges as he continues his narrative of the events that led to Sisera's demise,

> *Now Heber the Kenite had left the other Kenites,* the descendants of Hobab, Moses' brother-in-law, and pitched his tent by the great tree in Zaanannim near Kedesh. (Judg 4:11)

These words show us that,

PART 4 : PITFALLS AND PROGENY OF CHANGE

Heber the Kenite Had Broken His Alliance With General Sisera's Country!

> *Now Heber the Kenite had left the other Kenites...*

There it is in black and white: apparently, by moving away from his fellow Kenites, Heber had repudiated his alliance with Sisera's king—a fact which Sisera didn't seem to know. Not keeping abreast of this latest fact led to Sisera's death! In short, Sisera thought the alliance with Heber the Kenite still subsisted—big mistake! While it's highly unlikely that not keeping abreast of the facts will result in your physical death, the story of Sisera helps leaders everywhere see the dire importance of keeping tabs on things. *When it comes to navigating the uncertainty that always accompanies change, information—nay, the most current information—is king.* The more you can keep abreast of the facts of the matter, the better you can handle the fluidity that's always part of the change process.

RISK V RECKLESSNESS: WHEN IS MY ACTION RECKLESS?

King David of ancient Israel was one man who knew about risk. He risked his life when he singlehandedly fought off a lion that attacked the sheep he kept; he also risked his life in his unequal fight against Goliath and in the quelling of a military rebellion led by his own son Absalom. While the risks you may need to take today may not physically endanger you, they certainly can mess up your rice bowl (personal finances) and the quality of your relationships with other people. While most of us are averse to risk and don't want to have anything to do with it, for a sizeable minority, the question isn't whether risks should be borne, but how to differentiate risky actions from reckless ones. David, a man acquainted with risk, shows us just how to differentiate the risky from the reckless, saying,

> *Though I constantly take my life in my hands,* I will not forget your law. (Ps 119:109)

Managing the Uncertainty that Always Accompanies Change

Risk is Not Recklessness

David was continually taking risks, attempting new things and going up against obstacles far bigger than him and his resources; he was, as the saying goes, "constantly taking his life in his own hands." Who can forget how he took his life in his own hands and went up against Goliath? Yet, this passage of Scripture helps us see that his risk taking behavior was always bounded by God's law. In simple terms, while David was always ready to assume risk, he was also always guided in his actions by a core set of principles. When your risky behavior is not bounded by this same set of principles, you might just be straying into the realm of recklessness. So, '"What principles," you might ask, "must guide a person who bears risk and drives change?" The writer of Proverbs gives some answers, saying,

> The words of the reckless pierce like swords... (Prov 12:18)

Recklessness Openly Alienates Others

> The *words* of the *reckless* pierce like swords...

Did you notice that a key way to recognize a reckless person is to simply listen to his words: his words wantonly alienate even his closest allies. After all is said and done, *recklessness is an attitude that births action. Reckless persons are little concerned about the feelings and views of others, and they don't seek or value the input of others.* Every time you say things like, "I don't care what they think, I am going ahead to do what I want to do," or whenever you use speech that isn't *inclusive* ("That's none of *your* business."), you just might be treading on the boundaries of recklessness and whatever action you take at that time becomes reckless, not just risky.

Reckless People Don't Seek or Take Advice

> The *words of the reckless pierce like swords...*

In other words, reckless people are little concerned about the feelings and views of allies and other team members, and every word they speak shows it. Every time you find yourself eagerly discounting the views and advice of fellow leaders or co-travellers, you may have just stepped into "reckless territory."

PART 4 : PITFALLS AND PROGENY OF CHANGE

It's Reckless If It Can't Stand the Scrutiny of Teammates And Allies

The words of the reckless pierce like swords...

The underlying assumption of the words of the writer of Proverbs is that *a healthy risk is one that can pass the test of scrutiny by those closest to you.* You certainly are free to discount the advice of your inner circle, but you should always bear in mind the fact that a healthy risk is one that can pass the test of scrutiny of members of your inner circle. After all is said and done, the key signature of recklessness is that it doesn't seek the input of others.

The Case of President George W Bush and the Second Gulf War

In 2003 United States President George W. Bush ordered American troops to invade Iraq. Although the troops achieved the immediate objective of "conquering" that country and toppling the administration of Iraqi president Saddam Hussein, the situation subsequently spiraled out of control as an insurgency took root and gained widespread support from the locals. Thousands of American troops, and hundreds of thousands of Iraqi citizens perished in the wake of that insurgency. The truth is this: unlike the First Gulf War of the nineties (when then President George H. W. Bush—father of President George W. Bush—had sought and won the support of key allies), President George W. Bush ignored the advice of key allies like France and other members of the European Union. In fact, French president Jacque Chirac openly railed against the Second Gulf War. Many of President Bush's key officials—the so called neo cons—even concocted a doctrine that allowed them act without needing to seek the support of allies! Bush's decision to invade over the strident objections of key allies is, in retrospect, reckless.

Wrap Around

Implementing change is akin to opening a black box. And uncertainty is one thing that always pops out of the latter. Uncertainty is rooted in our ignorance and lack of knowledge, and reveals itself as an inability to control outcomes and results. Because uncertainty means that circumstances are fluid and volatile, managing uncertainty requires that leaders continuously cultivate the sources that can provide them with the latest information. In the language of the street, managing uncertainty demands that you keep

Managing the Uncertainty that Always Accompanies Change

your ear to the ground. One way leaders keep an ear to the ground is to value interruptions. The latter, because they allow for the injection of newer, timely, and task-relevant information into the decision-making process, are a primary way to manage uncertainty. Because uncertainty always births risk, effective change agents are those who are prepared to handle risk. Symmetric risk is managed by making multiple small bets, and by picking yourself up and pressing on after every failed attempt. Not so for asymmetric risk—where a single "bad luck" event can wipe out all previous gains. Asymmetric risk is managed by avoiding or not playing the game. Risk is more likely to become recklessness when it doesn't seek or take counsel from allies and teammates.

20

Last Word

NAVIGATING THE CHALLENGE OF CHANGE

RECALL THAT, IN HIS book, *The Principles and Benefits of Change*, motivational speaker Myles Munroe spoke about four types of change. He said that,

> We generally experience four types of change in life: (1) change that happens around us, (2) change that happens to us, (3) change that happens within us, and (4) change that we make happen.

He went on to describe each type of change, saying,

1. Change that happens to us—unexpected or anticipated change that affects our personal lives, families, careers, and so forth.

2. Change that happens around us—unexpected or anticipated change that affects our society, nation, or world and that also has some impact on us personally or on our ways of life.

3. Change that happens within us—unexpected or anticipated change that directly affects who we are—either physically, emotionally, mentally, or spiritually.

4. Change that we initiate—something created or altered by plans we have implemented in order to move us from the present to a preferred future.

We can identify each of the above as a distinct type of change, even though, sometimes, there may be overlap between them.

Last Word

In my opinion, the challenge associated with navigating Types 1 and 2 Change is a little different from that associated with Type 4 Change. The latter deals with change that you consciously initiate, while the former involves managing change that happens to, or around, you. In Type 4 Change you're in the driver's seat and already possess a rough idea of what needs to be done. In Types 1 and 2 Change you have to first become aware of the change itself—which, as we shall see, is a difficult thing—before you can correctly respond to it. In this sense, it's this 'awareness gap' or isolation from reality—when you don't even know that change is happening—that's at the heart of navigating Types 1 and 2 Change. Just take a look around and you'll see that the change that most negatively impacts us is often the one to which we are oblivious, unaware or even blind. Indeed, Nokia CEO Stephen Elop admitted that a key reason his company fell behind was that top management wasn't even aware of the changes occurring in mobile telephony (see the Case of Nokia, chapter 1). Therefore, the critical step in navigating Types 1 and 2 Change involves...

CONQUERING MANAGERIAL ISOLATION FROM REALITY

A deaf ear is the first sign of a closed mind.

—JOHN MAXWELL

In leadership, they say that the higher you go, the cooler it becomes. But the truth is a little more nuanced, and it's this; the higher you go, the more isolated from reality and cut off from the facts you're likely to become. Stanford professors Jeffrey Pfeffer and Robert Sutton, in their excellent book, *Hard Facts, Dangerous Half-truths and Total Nonsense,* drive this point home as they describe the similarities between the *Columbia* and *Challenger* space shuttle accidents...

> This is one of the reasons as news travels up the hierarchical levels, each messenger changes it a bit more to tell the boss a happier and happier story. This so called mum effect helps explain what Nobel Prize-winning physicist Richard Feynman learned when investigating the 1986 explosion of the Challenger space shuttle. Feynman asked a group of engineers to estimate the probability

that the shuttle's main engine would fail. Their estimates ranged from 1-in-200 to 1-in-300. When Feynmann asked NASA's boss to make the same estimate, he proposed a failure of 1-in-100,000. Feynmann estimated that this was one of the many illustrations that managerial isolation from reality was rampant throughout NASA, a problem that persisted after the Challenger explosion, according to the independent panel that studied why the Columbia shuttle disintegrated on re-entry in 2005.

These grim words help us see the grave dangers that managerial isolation from reality can cause. Indeed, that kind of isolation can also blind leaders from seeing the changes happening in their operating environment—hampering their ability to successfully navigate change. How can that happen? The writer of Proverbs shows us just how, saying,

> ... he who builds a high gate invites destruction. (Prov 17:19)

Managerial Isolation from Reality Invites Destruction

Notice carefully that this passage of Scripture doesn't say, "... he who builds a high *wall* invites destruction." It actually says that,

> ... he who builds a high *gate* invites destruction.

Since a gate is really only a door in a wall to regulate the flow of people into a compound, this passage is actually talking about the flow of people and the information they carry. Again, since poor and unsuccessful persons are unlikely to build high gates—the rich and the successful are more likely to do that—it means that insularity or managerial isolation from reality is more likely to occur among top-management. In effect, the higher you go in an organization, the more isolated from reality and cut off from the facts you're likely to become.

Leaders who build 'high gates' are people who, in any way, hamper the flow of information that reaches them. Not having the benefit of true and realistic information is what disconnects them from reality and sets them up for destruction. So how can you counter this tendency to build 'high gates', to become insular and disconnected from reality—things that blind people from being aware of the change that's happening to, and around, them? In other words, how can leaders keep their gates 'low'? The answers lie in the following three conscious actions...

1. Employ a devil's advocate: designate jobs whose occupants have the duty to bring up uncomfortable truths and the proverbial other side of the coin. These devil's advocates are paid and promoted for their ability to generate views that don't fit with other members of the team.
2. Learn to listen, and listen to learn. Avoid dominating conversations with others.
3. Develop close friendships with independent persons who can give you truthful feedback.

LEADING WHEN NO ONE IS FOLLOWING

It should be borne in mind that there is nothing more difficult to arrange, more doubtful of success and more dangerous to carry through than initiating changes. The innovator makes enemies of all those who prospered under the old order, and only lukewarm support is forthcoming from those who would prosper under the new.

—NICCOLO MACHIAVELLI

I am sure you've heard the old saw: he who thinks he's leading and has no one following is only taking a walk. The assumption underlying that adage is that the best leaders *always* have people following them. But, and this is crucial, navigating change often requires leaders who are willing—at least for some time—to lead when no one is following. This often happens at the beginning of an enterprise when few persons believe in your vision of change and when you've not yet generated the small wins needed to convince critics and affirm believers. So what does it take to lead when no one is following? What does it take to stand alone and against popular opinion? What does it take to start something when everyone thinks you are 'crazy' and will ultimately come to some grief? Interestingly, the answers to these questions are revealed by a close study of the life of one of ancient Israel's most vilified and most misunderstood leaders—Samson. Almost everyone knows that Samson was a 'one man army'—able to vanquish a thousand enemy soldiers with the simple jaw bone of a donkey. He's also notorious for his weakness—an inability to withstand the delicate charms of exotic women; a weakness that doomed his leadership and led to his death. But there was another side to Samson. Listen to the writer of Judges as he shows us that often ignored side. . .

> For, lo, thou shalt bear a son [Samson]; and no razor shall come on his head. . . he shall begin to deliver Israel from the hand of the Philistines. (Judg 13:5)

Samson was a Pioneer

> . . . he shall *begin* to deliver Israel from the hand of the Philistines.

Samson's purpose was clear: to *begin*—not to complete or continue—the deliverance of Israel from the hand of a militarily entrenched enemy. In this sense, he was a pioneer— attempting to do what no one else had ever done. At his death, he had accomplished that mission—making a huge dent on the Philistine power structure by wiping out all her leaders. The question becomes: what specific qualities enabled Samson to move almost single-handedly against the might of Israel's Philistine overlords? The answer, as usual, lies hidden in the words of the writer of 'Judges. . .

> Then the Philistines went up and camped in Judah. . . The men of Judah asked, "Why have you come to fight us?" "We have come to take Samson prisoner, they answered, "to do to him as he did to us." Then three thousand men of Judah went down. . . and said to Samson, "Don't you realize that the Philistines are rulers over us? What have you done to us?. . . We will tie you and hand you over to them. . . (Judg 15: 7-12)

At the Beginning of an Enterprise, Change Often Challenges the Leader to Stand Alone; to Display Courage

Samson had to fight his numerous battles with the Philistine enemy alone; his string of victories didn't sway any of his countrymen to join him, and not once did he receive help and encouragement from the people he served. In fact, in this passage, we see a three-thousand-strong army of Judah tie him up and deliver him to the Philistines! Samson's leadership illustrates the dilemma that pioneering leaders everywhere must face: because their way is not proven, they must be willing to act alone initially, and to also suffer misunderstanding and even opposition from friends and compatriots who paradoxically stand to benefit from their actions. In this sense, Samson's leadership mirrors the burden that entrepreneurs, inventors, innovators and those at the cutting edge of change must bear. No wonder James Kouzes and Barry Posner in their excellent book, *The Leadership Challenge*, said that,

> Leaders are pioneers. They are people who venture into unexplored territory. They guide us to new and unfamiliar destinations... [they]... move us forward. Leaders get us going someplace.

To do all this they must, at some point, be ready to lead when no one is following; to follow the courage of their own convictions.

Courage is often the Result of a Commitment to a Higher Cause

So where does 'courage' come from? The word 'courage' is derived from the French word 'coeur', which literally means heart, and can be translated as commitment. The root of Samson's courage lay in his commitment to a higher cause—to God's plan for his life. For British Prime Minister Winston Churchill, who displayed unusual courage during World War 2; the higher cause was his hatred of evil, as biographer William Manchester writes in *The Last Lion*,

> Long before his countrymen understood the Nazi challenge, Winston[Churchill] realized that Hitler was the very embodiment of evil.

Churchill's Manichean perspective meant that he was never ready to negotiate with anything he considered evil; a thing which fueled his willingness to stand alone, if necessary.

The writer of Judges continues his discourse on Samson's leadership, saying,

> The Philistines went up and camped in Judah, spreading out near Lehi. The men of Judah asked, "Why have you come to fight us?" "We have come to take Samson prisoner," they answered,... Then three thousand men from Judah went down to the cave in the rock of Etam and said to Samson, "Don't you realize that the Philistines are rulers over us? What have you done to us?"... So they bound him with two new ropes... (Judg 15:7-12)

This depressing account of Samson's battle with the Philistine army and, wait for it, the crass willingness of Judah's soldiers (three thousand of them) to hand him over unconditionally to the enemy only serve to let us know that. . .

At the Beginning, a Change Agent is Often 'Hated' by the Old Order and Receives Lukewarm Support from People who Stand to Benefit from her Actions

Life can be lonely for a change agent. Although Samson had begun to destroy the main infrastructure of oppression of the Philistines—their army—here we see an armed force of 3000 soldiers of Judah (Israel) negotiate with the Philistines and then, horror of horrors, bind Samson with ropes and deliver him to the enemy! The words of Italian scholar Niccolo Machiavelli ring true in this case,

> . . . The innovator makes enemies of all those who prospered under the old order, and only lukewarm support is forthcoming from those who would prosper under the new.

Predictably, the Philistines who prospered under the old order Samson wanted to overthrow, vehemently opposed him. But his own countrymen, who would have benefited fom the new order of things, were lukewarm—even conniving with the enemy to undercut him.

A Change Agent must Expect to be Lonely and Misunderstood

That Samson must have been lonely can be inferred from this fact: his string of miraculous victories against the Philistine enemy never convinced a single citizen of Israel to rally to his side! That he was misunderstood is inferred from another fact: at his death—when he'd killed off the whole leadership cadre of the enemy Philistines—only his brothers and close family attended his funeral (Judges 16:30-31). And he was Israel's judge and leader for a whole twenty years! Samson scored victory after victory against the Philistines, yet no one in Israel stood up to lend him a helping hand. I believe it was this loneliness—in addition to his character flaws—that made him exquisitely vulnerable to the wiles of conniving women like Delilah. But the writer of Judges isn't through with illustrating the challenge of change through the leadership of Samson; he goes on to say that,

> Samson went down to Timnah [the heartland of Philistia] and saw a woman there. . . His father and mother said, "Isn't there

an *acceptable* woman among your relatives and among all your people? Must you go to the uncircumcised Philistines to get a wife?" But Samson said to his father, "Get her for me. She's the right one for me." (Judg 14:1-3)

The Best Change Agents are Persons with a Low Need for Positive Affirmation from Others

In the communal culture of the Near East, people got married only when the proposed spouse was acceptable to other members of the family. In other words, marriage was really a group decision—a decision one takes in conjunction with close family members—and not an individual decision. But by saying that,

> Isn't there an *acceptable* woman among your relatives and among all your people? Must you go to the uncircumcised Philistines to get a wife?

The writer of Judges helps us see that Samson was willing to buck this important tradition. In effect, Samson was a man who needed little or no affirmation from others—a man who could live with public disapproval.

Like I said at the beginning of this chapter, navigating Type 4 Change—the change you initiate—often requires that you act alone for some time if necessary. This means that the best change agents are people with very low needs for affirmation from others; people who can chart their own course in the face of a disbelieving or credulous public. If you're a pioneer or change agent, then you must let this truth forge some steel into your spine and prepare you for the inevitable challenges ahead. To develop and/or determine the strength of your 'change muscles', ask yourself the following questions:

- When last did you take a different view or position from the rest of the crowd?
- When last did you go ahead with a project in spite of the misgivings of close members of your team or family?

PART 4 : PITFALLS AND PROGENY OF CHANGE

Wrap Around

All change is not the same. Types 1 and 2 Change is change that happens to, and around, us. Navigating those kinds of change begins with becoming aware of their occurrence—with conquering managerial isolation. Managerial isolation grows as leaders are promoted up the proverbial corporate ladder and become increasingly disconnected from the reality that happens at the front lines. Conquering managerial isolation requires you to build 'low gates'—to deliberately increase the flow and diversity of your information sources. In contrast, navigating Type 4 Change—the change that you initiate—requires courage and a willingness to stand alone for some time. For this type of change, the greatest challenges occur at the beginning, before you generate the small wins and develop the credibility needed to win support. They occur when no is willing to believe you, when even those who'd benefit from the proposed change are lukewarm, and when those who'd be hurt by it are openly hostile. While the challenges associated with Type 4 Change often occur during implementation, those associated with Types 1 and 2 often begin to occur well before implementation.

www.ingramcontent.com/pod-product-compliance
Lightning Source LLC
Chambersburg PA
CBHW051049160426
43193CB00010B/1117